iQuilt

contents

departments

02 note from irene

04 contributors

05 designer profiles
Linda Tiano and Linda Lum DeBono
spring the unexpected on us.

06 istyle
Perfect synergy. 3 takes on a classic.

18 iwonder
The creative life—notes on living it
and working it for all you've got.

19 iread
Book reviews—the best new releases
from Leisure Arts (and our competitors!).

19 icare
Put your favorite hobby to good use.

features

08 Smart Girls Do
Quick bags and an easy belt worth
reading about.

14 Blue Notes
When nothing conventional will do.

20 Baby Bloom
Nobody puts Baby in the corner.

25 project instructions
59 general instructions
68 insight
Our parting (inspirational) thought.

ON THE COVER: Photography by Jason Masters • Styling by Angela Alexander

a note from irene
Up For Anything

I know you. You're a study in contrasts–Ms. Nonconformity, Ms. she-who-will-never-go-along-to-get-along. Why, you're that square peg I'm always hearing so much about!

And it's a pleasure to meet you.

Because I've heard that you're always on the lookout for something new–a better coffeemaker, a quicker route to work, a hairstyle that suits your face shape but doesn't take all morning to perfect (good luck with that one). And that goes for your quilting projects as well. You want–you need that little extra something like an unexpected color or unpredictable pattern–you know, just to keep it real.

Lucky for you, that's exactly what we were going for with Designers' Mix.

We called in a couple of favors and convinced Linda Tiano and Linda Lum DeBono, two of today's most innovative quilt designers, to mix it up together in the same publication. And just as that was getting interesting, our own in-house designers waded in. The final result is a no-holds-barred, all-out quilt designer throw-down. Everybody brings their A-game. Everybody goes away a winner.

Especially you. You're always a winner. ∎

~Irene

Find free patterns, more information about our articles, countless tips for every day, and read my daily blog. It's our new website and we built it just for you. Find it at i-createit.com.

LET US KNOW WHAT YOU THINK!
Email at Retail_Marketing@LeisureArts.com and tell us your thoughts on iQuilt, ideas, tips, or any project photos you want to share!

The ideas come from the books...

It's fashion for you.
EXCLUSIVELY YOU

You can pick your favorite **knit**, **crochet**, **felting** or **sewing** projects from 8 instruction books. You'll love our coordinating purse handles, panels of faux leather and mock croc, embellishments, and purse hardware.

you can use fabric, knit or crochet!

we offer purse handles & hardware

accent with ribbons, buttons, mock croc, faux leather, or a ready-to-wear pin!

Quilted Double-Handle Satchel
from *Easy Fabric Purses* #4228

contributors

deb moore

...Director of Craft Publications, oversees the titles in the craft category, but admits that she'd almost always rather be writing than overseeing, so she was overjoyed to contribute to the i-titles. "Let's see—me, getting paid to have my say? Why wouldn't I want to?" Deb has a BA in Communications and an MA in English.

cheryl johnson

...is the Director of Quilt, Knit, and Crochet Publications and a dedicated stash-builder. A BA in English, a Master's degree in Business Administration, and an obsessively crafty personality make Leisure Arts the perfect place for Cheryl to spend her days. Her evenings are spent in the company of her Material Girl alter-ego: intrepid blogger, budding photographer, and lover of four-legged beasts.

lisa lancaster

...has a degree in Home Economics Education, but learned everything she knows about sewing from her mother. And even though her grandmother once observed that it made no sense to take perfectly good fabric, cut it into tiny pieces, and then sew it all back together again, Lisa credits both mother and grandmother for inspiring her love for the challenges of quilting.

frances huddleston

..."A few years ago, my boss came to me and took me to see her boss. I felt like I was being taken to the principal's office." But Frances wasn't headed for detention–she was being transferred to the Quilt Department. "What a break! I still love it!" Her degree is in Elementary Education (her mother was also a teacher) which may explain why she writes instructions for a living.

jean lewis

...has a thing for cloth. As a child, Jean remembers wishing for fabric instead of toys and learning to sew at about the same time the rest of us were learning to read. Jean has been quilting for almost 20 years, and has taught quilting, sewing, smocking, and other crafts.

ISBN-13: 978-1-60140-632-3
ISBN-10: 1-60140-632-0

Linda LumDeBono

KEEPING IT FRESH

When you want fresh ideas and modern color, you want designs by Linda Lum DeBono. "I'm always looking for the next thing in fashion," says Linda. "I like to stay just ahead of the trend. New colors always seem a little bit 'out there' or even a little crazy, but they can also be more subtle, while the style itself leans toward the fashion-forward end of the scale. The best look is one that expresses what's hot without going over the top."

When Linda isn't drawing bold new patterns or spending time with her husband, Reno, and their two young sons, she can be found working on textile designs. Her most recent line of fabrics by Henry Glass & Company features a dynamic blend of geometric and floral prints in exciting new hues.

All this design activity makes it hard to believe that Linda hasn't always known how to apply scissors and thread to fabric. Linda discovered her creative skills when Reno's employment brought their family to New Jersey from Canada, and Linda left behind a career in the pharmaceuticals industry. To stay busy, the young mom took a couple of quilt classes and discovered a new passion for sewing and designing. These days, Linda's work can be seen in a variety of crafting magazines and books.

To see more examples of Linda's creations, visit www.lindalumdebono.com. And to find additional Leisure Arts publications featuring Linda's distinctive flair for shape and color, check with your local retailer or go to www.leisurearts.com. ■

by Susan McManus Johnson

Linda Tiano

DESIGN EVOLUTION

"A project turns out the way it wants to be," says Linda Tiano. "I may start with a particular idea about how it's going to look, but I find that a project will make its own path. It's always fun to see the results, especially with today's new fabrics."

An example of this design-as-you-go method is the quilt on page 16. "The quilt started off just brown and turquoise, then I found the big floral fabric. When I saw that particular fabric, I knew it was right for this modern quilt. It introduced more color and brought the quilt to life."

There was one project in this collection that Linda says didn't happen in the usual way. "The apron design on page 7 came to me in my sleep," Linda laughs. "I didn't have to sit down and think about it—I actually just dreamed up the idea of using napkins and making the apron how it appears."

Linda's years of sewing and designing for Leisure Arts have produced creations from the whimsical to the sublime. These include home décor items and holiday gifts that have wowed us with their originality. In fact, Linda is so good at inventing new concepts that we were surprised to learn that her sewing skills were born of necessity and not the desire to be creative.

Linda states simply. "I had to make clothes for my three children. For me, the really fun part of sewing began about a decade later, when the quilt boom started. These days, I'm an active member of a quilt guild and three smaller quilting groups. But I sew all kinds of projects, and I like coming up with new ones. I even have a room dedicated as a work space. It's at the front of my house, where I can look out the window at my flowers and watch people go by."

When she isn't dreaming up new patterns or watching them evolve through the design process, Linda sews for her grandchildren. "I have nine grandkids, and I'm making sure they each have a quilt from me."

We won't be surprised if one of those quilts includes a large and colorful floral print. ■

by Susan McManus Johnson

multiple**APRON**personality

If one of the things that drive you to sew is your love for variety,
then you already know that one is not necessarily enough (of anything).
That was our thinking when we asked Linda Lum DeBono, Linda Tiano, and
our own in-house designers to give us their take on an old standby.

Some days you can't wait to get into the kitchen. Others—well, you just want to heat it up and go. Whatever your personality type, you gotta eat. And even though your moods may be complicated, these aprons definitely aren't.

COSMOPOLITAN

The Leisure Arts designers went with sophisticated dots and stripes (along with a bit of grosgrain) because no one ever accused you of being the domestic type. Give it a try and you're all set to fire up the fondue (or maybe just twist the lemons).

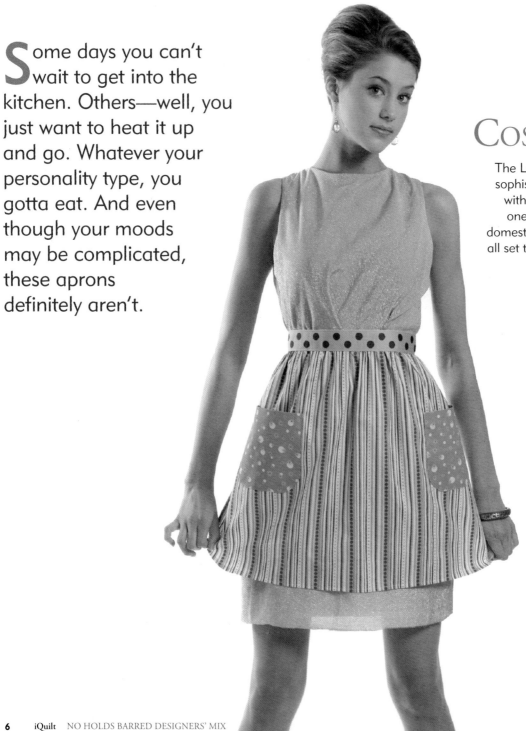

VIVE LE NAPPERON!

If you've got no stash to spare, Linda Tiano says, "Dig out those ridiculously expensive linen napkins you received as a wedding present." The bonus? Absolutely no hemming required.

THE COQUETTE

Mix and MATCH? Forget it. The more mixed the better. Linda Lum DeBono added a pleated ruffle for a flirty skirt effect.

SMART GIRLS DO

You're all about a room stuffed with musty old books, because that's all a girl like you needs to transport to another time or place. Use that great imagination of yours to re-think the construction of some of life's little necessities.

Add store-bought handles and a couple of seams to turn a beaded, linen placemat into a crisp tote for your travels through the canon.

Get your lit fix while you sew. Find links to free audio book podcasts at *i-createit.com*.

It's a good thing plain Jane Austen didn't think to whip up this cute little yo-yo belt—she might have spent more time out showing it off than practicing good sense and sensibility. And that would have been a tragedy.

You don't mind getting lost in a good story, but you hate it when you can't find your lipstick. This little clutch is the perfect size when you're taking just the essentials (like a little spare change for overdue fines).

THE CELTIC RING

undamentals of
AL INVESTIGATION

947-1952

TALK

Obviously, you've got more going for you than mere book smarts. Who else would know that a black satin cord is all that's required to turn a modern, graphic placemat into a bag that really does go with everything?

Don't be such a smarty-pants. It's a tassel, a bit of cord, and a placemat. No need to write a book report on it.

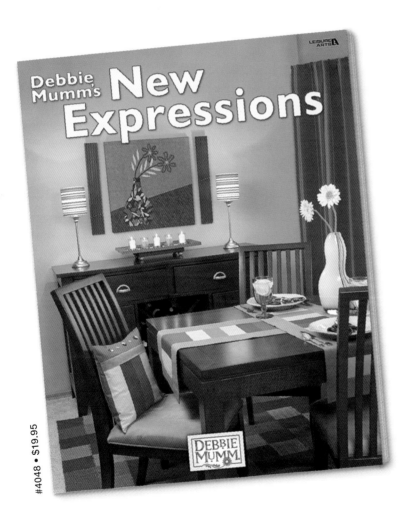

blue
notes

Yo! Quilt

If a bright blue wall is your idea of the perfect visual treat—if you never met a piece of cast-off furniture you didn't like—if you believe that there's not a lot a vase of fresh flowers can't put right, then you totally get this giant yo-yo quilt.

love you

friends

believe

what's not to like?

All the little things you need to hear, just when you
need to hear them. Appliqué, embroider, and
stamp on puffed-up throw pillows to soften the blow.
Stack em up, the world can be a hard place.

Where's everybody going?

Oh, come on. You knew there would be at least one design that would make you run straight to your stash or the fabric store. Admit it. You're imagining your version of this design-as-you-go quilt right now.

LET GO OF PERFECT

If you're like me, your love affair with color began at an early age, before the worries of perspective, realism, and the "real" world impacted your idea of what art could be. Do you remember the inspiration of a blank sheet of paper and a brand new box of crayons, the points still sharp and the world full of choices of things to be drawn? I liked purple horses, yellow suns, and stick figures posed carefully in front of a blue house with a red roof and a huge tree made up of swirly leaves and a thin brown trunk. Today I don't have much opportunity to play with crayons and imagination. Today it's all about fabric...and imagination.

Now, you and I, we're all grown up or we're supposed to be. And that means thinking long and hard about what color is "right" when we're creating. In fact, we spend a lot of time choosing the "right" fabrics. This is my favorite part of quilting, playing with fabric, organizing, auditioning, buying more, re-organizing, planning, and then cutting. I like beginnings, fresh starts, projects that haven't had the first wrong cut or imperfect point. Each new start is the opportunity

to produce the perfect quilt. Of course, when I was drawing my purple horse, there was no question of whether or not it was perfect. Of course it was. It was exactly what I imagined!

We might never find a home on the walls of our family room for a quilt with a purple horse or family portrait of stick figures, but think of how much fun we would have building a quilt entirely from imagination. Forgetting precise points and the science of the color wheel and forging ahead with something that's uniquely you. Can you do it? Can I? Most quilters love the precision and the satisfaction of producing the "perfect" quilt... perfectly pieced, perfectly quilted, perfectly bound, and hung in the absolutely perfect place. Others, like me, just keep trying to get there, to reach perfection on the next project.

Every crayon drawing of mine was prominently displayed using refrigerator magnets in the heart of our home...the kitchen. It wasn't real, it wasn't "right", but it was art to at least one person. Let go of "perfect." Stretch yourself and remember the feeling of no limits... a blank page and a fresh box of crayons. ∎ *by Cheryl Johnson*

Stretch yourself and remember the feeling of no limits.

GIVE 'EM A STITCH
and they'll make you SMILE

DEBBIE MUMM'S NEW EXPRESSIONS

So how about a little textile décor designed for those of us who crave sophistication? Debbie Mumm knows how to put fabric on a pedestal. And on a table, wall, or bed, for that matter. Witness the color-punch table runners, the striped pillows, and the just-for-fun artwork in this New Expressions collection. Debbie approached the creation of this decorator ensemble with seven distinct themes in mind, but you can easily apply your own themes by changing fabric colors. Feel free to make your shelves, desk and chair, storage boxes, lamp, and chandelier shine from your own particular perspective.

New Expressions, Leisure Arts, Inc. • $19.95 • Leisure Arts Leaflet #4048 • www.leisurearts.com

CRAZY FOR BABY

Need a gift for a member of the diaper set? If you haven't discovered the wild and crazy quilts dreamed up by Me & My Sister Designs, be sure to sneak a peek at these neon-bright quilted confections for infants and toddlers. Any youngster will trade in her lollipop for a nap if it means snuggling up in one of these colorful designs. In fact, we suspect there may be several adults who wouldn't mind borrowing one of the quilts to catch forty on the sofa. Come to think of it, these simple shapes would also work great with those oversize decorator prints that are popping up everywhere. So why not make a blankie for Baby with kittens or cars, then treat yourself to a lap quilt that will look right on your sofa? Nobody has to know it came from a baby book, even one this adorable.

Crazy for Baby, Leisure Arts, Inc. • $10.95 • Leisure Arts Leaflet #4161 • www.leisurearts.com

THE IMPATIENT EMBROIDERER

You know that little creative itch that starts up whenever you see decorative stitches on clothing, linens, handbags, and whatnot? If lack of time or experience has you reticent to scratch, here's your incentive to really go after it. Author Jayne Emerson has a soothingly practical take on teaching the basics of embroidery for hand and machine stitching. Her instructions and hand-drawn illustrations are easy to follow. But don't expect any sunbonnet girls or dancing vegetables to show up in these 112 pages. Jayne has a good take on what modern stitchers really want—funky, friendly embellishments they can use in real life.

The Impatient Embroiderer, Potter Craft • $22.95 • www.crownpublishing.com • www.clarksonpotter.com

icare   Newborns In Need

Few charities can tug on the heartstrings like this one! Newborns In Need is a non-profit organization that gives much-needed baby supplies to new parents who live in low-income areas or who are unprepared for the arrival of their child. Blankets, quilts, clothing, pacifiers, baby powder, diapers, and many other baby items are among the items Newborns In Need provides. And monetary donations are always welcome. For the price of a candy bar, the organization is able to purchase one of several useful items. Visit www.newbornsinneed.org to learn about the many ways you can help the smallest children have a better start in life.

BABY *bloom*

Just because you're about to be a new mom doesn't mean your sense of style has to go on maternity leave. Show the new kid on the block that you still know a thing or two about what's cool.

Remember—she's new, and depending on you to show her everything she needs to know about color, style, and flair. Hang easy fabric-covered canvases especially designed to appeal to the baby-hipster aesthetic.

Pink or blue might be new to the kid in the
diaper, but you've pretty much seen it. Pacify the
urge to surge with vibrant orange, red, teal, and
turquoise bumper pads, crib quilt and dust ruffle.

Thank goodness, Mama's got a brand new bag. When you're both awake (but only one of you wants to be) having the toys (and binkey) within easy reach might just save the day.

Need more nursery ideas? Go to *i-createit.com*.

He's short, fat, and bald—and you'd follow him anywhere. Just don't forget that he's going to need some hang time with his peeps. Flowered turtle and dotted stripe bunny (a.k.a. the Tortoise and the Hare) are the perfect naptime companions.

Discover a
Garden
of FRESH IDEAS

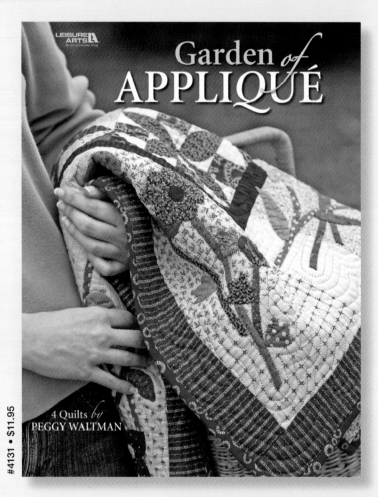

#4131 • $11.95

Garden *of*
APPLIQUÉ

4 Quilts *by*
PEGGY WALTMAN

You won't need a green thumb to **cultivate these creative florals**. Just grab your **quilting tools** and **dig deep in your fabric stash** because **Peggy Waltman's** appliquéd blooms are sure to **inspire you to grow a beautiful garden in fabric**.

THE COQUETTE APRON

shown on page 7

YARDAGE REQUIREMENTS

Yardage is based on 43"/44" (109 cm/112 cm) wide fabric with a "usable width" of 40" (102 cm).

- ⁵/₈ yd (57 cm) of green print #1
- ¹/₈ yd (11 cm) *each* of green print #2 and green print #3 fabrics
- ³/₈ yd (34 cm) *each* of brown print #1 and brown print #2 fabrics
- ¹/₈ yd (11 cm) of brown print #3 fabric

You will also need:

- 4" x 21¹/₂" (10 cm x 55 cm) rectangle of paper for pattern

CUTTING OUT THE PIECES

Follow Rotary Cutting, page 59, to cut fabric.

From green print #1 fabric:
- Cut 1 **apron lining** 21¹/₂" x 18¹/₄".
- Cut 1 **rectangle** 4" x 16¹/₂".

From *each* of green print #2 and green print #3 fabrics:
- Cut 1 **rectangle** 4" x 16¹/₂".

From brown print #1 fabric:
- Cut 1 **waistband** 4" x 21¹/₂".
- Cut 1 **ruffle** 7" x 26".

From brown print #2 fabric:
- Cut 2 **ties** 3¹/₂" x 25".
- Cut 2 **rectangles** 4" x 16¹/₂".

From brown print #3 fabric:
- Cut 1 **rectangle** 4" x 16¹/₂".

MAKING THE APRON

Follow Machine Piecing, page 59, and Pressing, page 60. Use ¹/₄" seam allowances throughout.

1. To make pattern for waistband, match short edges and fold paper in half to find center. Measure 2¹/₄" from top corners on each short end; mark. Draw bottom edge as shown in **Fig. 1**. Cut along drawn line, slightly rounding point at center bottom.

2. Use pattern to trim bottom edge of **waistband**.

3. Sew 6 **rectangles** together to make apron **skirt**. Pin bottom edge of waistband pattern over top edge of **skirt** (**Fig. 2**) and trim along bottom edge of pattern.

4. Matching centers and right sides, pin bottom edge of **waistband** to top edge of **skirt**. Pivoting as needed at curve, sew **waistband** to **skirt** to make **apron front**.

5. Matching right sides and long raw edges, fold **ruffle** in half. Sew short sides. Clip corners and turn **ruffle** right side out. Randomly fold pleats in **ruffle** so that **ruffle** measures 21" wide. Baste across top raw edges of **ruffle** to hold pleats in place; set aside.

6. Press 1 short edge and long edges of each **tie** ¹/₄" to wrong side. Matching wrong sides, press **ties** in half lengthwise. Stitch along folded edges.

7. Matching right sides and raw edges and placing **ruffle** ¹/₄" from side edges of **apron front**, baste **ruffle** to bottom edge of **apron front**. Matching right sides and raw edges, baste **ties** to **waistband** ³/₈" from top edge.

8. Pin **ruffle** and **ties** away from seamlines so they do not get caught when stitching. Matching right sides, sew **apron front** and **lining** together, leaving an opening for turning along 1 side edge. Clip corners and turn apron right side out. Sew opening closed.

Design by Linda Lum DeBono

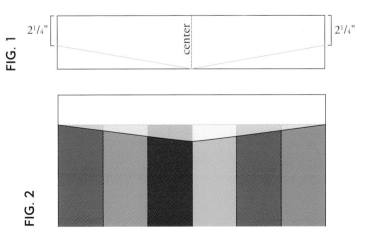

FIG. 1

FIG. 2

instructions

COSMOPOLITAN APRON

shown on page 6

YARDAGE REQUIREMENTS

Yardage is based on 43"/44"
(109 cm/112 cm) wide fabric with
a "usable width" of 40" (102 cm).

    $^5/_8$ yd (57 cm) of cream stripe
    fabric

    $^1/_4$ yd (23 cm) of turquoise print
    fabric

You will also need:

    3 yds (2.7 m) of $1^1/_2$" (38 mm)
    wide grosgrain or satin ribbon

CUTTING OUT THE PIECES

Follow **Rotary Cutting**, *page 59, to cut fabric.*

From cream stripe fabric:

• Cut 1 **apron skirt** 30" x 19".

From turquoise print fabric:

• Cut 2 **pockets** 7" x 8".

MAKING THE APRON

Follow **Machine Piecing**, *page 59, and* **Pressing**, *page 60.*

1. Using a plate approximately 10" in diameter as pattern, round corners on 1 long edge of **apron skirt** (**Fig. 1**).

2. In the same manner, use a cup or glass approximately 4" in diameter as pattern to round corners on 1 short edge of each **pocket**.

3. Stitch around **apron skirt** on sides and bottom $^1/_2$" from raw edges. Press hem on side and bottom edges, pressing under $^1/_4$" twice and using stitching as guide. Topstitch hem in place.

4. Press top edge of **apron skirt** $^1/_4$" to *right* side.

5. Machine stitch basting lines approximately $^1/_{16}$", $^3/_8$", and $1^3/_4$" from top folded edge of **apron skirt**. Gather top edge to 20".

6. Center and sew ribbon over gathers $^1/_8$" from edges of ribbon. Cut ribbon ends to desired length.

7. For each **pocket**, press top edge $^1/_2$" to wrong side. Stitch hem in place along fold. Press top edge of **pocket** 1" to *right* side. Stitch around pocket on sides and bottom $^1/_2$" from edges. Clip corners and turn top edge right side out. Press **pocket**, using stitching as guide to press raw edges to wrong side.

8. Arrange **pockets** on apron as desired and topstitch in place.

Design by L.A. Staff

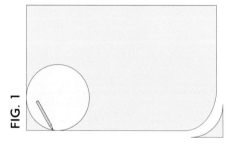

FIG. 1

VIVE LE NAPPERON! APRON

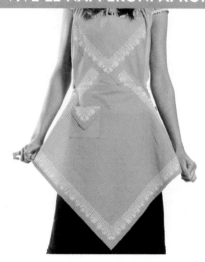

SUPPLIES

    2 cloth napkins 20" x 20"
    (51 cm x 51 cm)

    3 yds (2.7 m) of $^5/_8$" (16 mm)
    wide coordinating grosgrain
    ribbon

MAKING THE APRON

Note: Red dashed lines on **Figs.** *indicate stitching lines; blue solid lines indicate cutting lines.*

1. To make **bib**, lay 1 napkin on flat surface, right side down. Referring to **Fig. 1**, fold 2 opposite corners to wrong side so that width measures 11". Stitch points of folded corners.

2. Referring to **Fig. 2**, fold top corner to wrong side to form flap that measures $9^3/_4$". Stitch through all layers along sides and bottom edges of flap. Cut bottom corner of napkin off $1^1/_4$" below point of flap. (Set aside cut piece of napkin for pocket.)

quilt tip

Before stitching ribbon to apron, cut a strip of paper-backed fusible web slightly narrower than ribbon and 20" long. Place strip over gathers on right side of apron skirt; press in place. Remove paper and place ribbon over web; press in place.

3. On remaining napkin, measure from 1 corner 7$^1/_2$" in both directions; cut corner to make **skirt** (**Fig. 3**).

4. Matching right side of **skirt** to side of **bib** with flap and aligning raw edges, sew **skirt** and **bib** together using 1" seam allowance (**Fig. 4**).

5. Cut two 30" lengths of ribbon. Placing ribbon ends on seam allowance of **skirt**, machine stitch ends to seam allowances (**Fig. 5**).

6. Press raw edges of seam allowances $^1/_4$" toward **skirt**. Press entire seam allowances toward **skirt** and sew in place. Sew ribbons in place at side edges of **skirt** (**Fig. 6**).

7. Tie apron around waist to determine desired length for neck ribbon. Add 3" to determined length. Press each end of ribbon $^3/_4$" to wrong side. Overlapping **bib** by $^3/_4$", sew ribbon ends to wrong side and top edge of **bib** (**Fig. 6**).

8. Using piece cut from **bib**, press corner 3" to wrong side. Cut a 5" x 5" square as shown in **Fig. 7**.

9. Press raw edges of **pocket** $^1/_2$" to right side. Pin **pocket**, flap side out, to apron skirt and topstitch in place approximately $^1/_{16}$" from side and bottom edges.

Design by Linda Turno

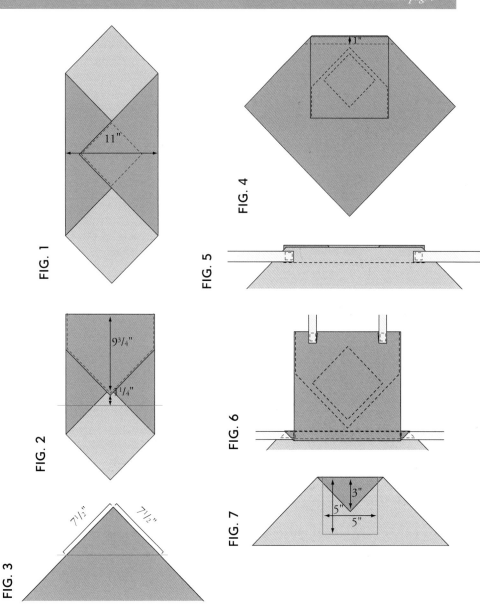

FIG. 1

FIG. 2

FIG. 3

FIG. 4

FIG. 5

FIG. 6

FIG. 7

quilt tip

Personalize your apron by embroidering or stamping your initials on the bib and pocket, or dress it up with fringe sewn along the flaps of the bib and pocket.

instructions

TRAVELING PURSE
shown on page 8

MAKING THE PURSE

1. Matching wrong sides and short edges, fold placemat in half. Machine stitch sides through both layers as shown by red dashed lines in **Fig. 1**.
2. Fold top beaded edge $1^{1}/_{4}$" to right side (**Fig. 2**).
3. From cotton fabric scrap, cut 4 strips $1^{1}/_{4}$" x $2^{3}/_{4}$". Press all raw edges of strips $^{1}/_{4}$" to wrong side; press strips in half lengthwise. Place 1 strip through each handle ring and tack ends of strip to purse as shown in **Purse Diagram**.

FIG. 2

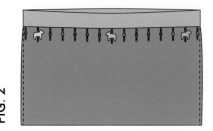

PURSE DIAGRAM

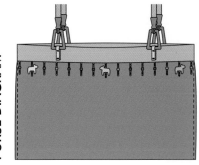

Design by Linda Tiano

SUPPLIES

1 placemat with beads
on short edges
Scrap of matching
cotton fabric
1 pair of purchased
purse handles

FIG. 1

YO-YO BELT
shown on page 9

FINISHED BELT SIZE:
79" (201 cm) long

YARDAGE REQUIREMENTS
*Yardage is based on 43"/44"
(109 cm/112 cm) wide fabric with
a "usable width" of 40" (102 cm).*
$^{1}/_{4}$ yd (23 cm) of black print fabric
$^{3}/_{8}$ yd (34 cm) of red floral fabric

MAKING THE BELT

1. From black print fabric, cut 2 strips 3" x 40". Using $^{1}/_{4}$" seam allowance, sew strips together, end to end, to make 1 continuous strip for belt. Cut belt to desired length.
2. Press all edges of belt $^{1}/_{4}$" to wrong side. With wrong sides together, fold belt in half lengthwise and stitch around folded edges.
3. Using yo-yo pattern, page 31, cut 12 circles from red floral fabric. Follow **Making Yo-Yos**, page 61, to make 12 yo-yos. Beginning in center of belt, tack yo yos to belt.

Design by Linda Lum DeBono

GOES-WITH-EVERYTHING PURSE

shown on page 11

SUPPLIES

1 placemat
1 yd (91 cm) of ⁵/₁₆" (8 mm)
    diameter matching twisted
    satin cord
Chalk pencil
Thick, clear drying craft glue

MAKING THE PURSE

Note: Yellow dashed lines on **Figs.** indicate stitching lines.

1. Matching wrong sides and long edges, fold placemat in half. Find horizontal center by folding placemat in half; mark center with chalk pencil. Machine stitch sides and center through all layers as shown in **Fig. 1**.

2. Stitch top edge from center to edge of placemat (**Fig. 2**).

3. Keeping edge stitched in Step 2 on top and matching short ends, fold placemat in half. Move back layer out of the way and stitch near top edge through remaining layers as shown in **Fig. 3**.

4. Fold placemat in half and stitch through all layers near side and bottom edges as shown in **Fig. 4**.

5. Fold open top left corner to make flap and tack flap to 3rd layer only (make sure not to catch back layer).

6. Cut cord to desired length and use glue to prevent cord ends from raveling. (**Note:** _It may help to wrap rubber bands around cord ends while glue is drying._) Once glue has dried, make rosette by curling 1 cord end and using needle and thread to tack cord together. Tie knot in remaining end of cord. Tack knotted end to inside of purse (between 3rd and back layers) and rosette end to front of 3rd layer (make sure not to catch back layer).

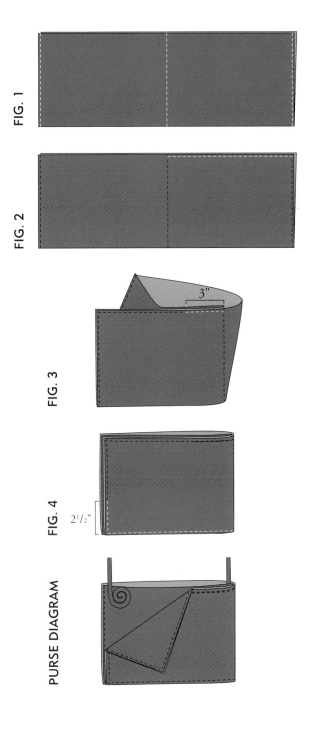

FIG. 1

FIG. 2

FIG. 3

FIG. 4

2¹/₂"

3"

PURSE DIAGRAM

Design by Linda Tiano

instructions

ESSENTIALS CLUTCH

FINISHED CLUTCH SIZE:
Approximately 9" x 6" (23 cm x 15 cm)

YARDAGE REQUIREMENTS
Yardage is based on 43"/44" (109 cm/112 cm) wide fabric with a "usable width" of 40" (102 cm).
  $1/4$ yd (23 cm) *each* of pink print and green print fabrics
  Scrap *each* of brown floral and gold floral print fabric
  $1/4$ yd (23 cm) of fabric for lining
You will also need:
  Two 8" x 12" (20 cm x 30 cm) pieces of batting
  1 sew-on snap
  Letter-size piece of paper for pattern

MAKING THE YO-YO PURSE

Use $1/4$" seam allowances throughout. Clutch and yo-yo patterns are on page 31.

1. Cut 1 **rectangle** 8" x 20" from *each* of pink print and green print fabrics. For **front/back**, match right sides and sew **rectangles** together along 1 long side.

2. Aligning raw edges, layer batting and **front/back** (right side up). Follow **Quilting**, page 61, to baste and quilt as desired. Our clutch is meander quilted.

3. With green fabric on *right* side and with crease line aligned with seamline, place clutch pattern on right side of **front/back**; cut **front**. Repeat with green fabric on *left* side to cut **back**.

4. Matching short ends, fold fabric for lining in half. Using clutch pattern, cut 2 **linings**.

5. Referring to pattern, make tucks in bottom corners of **front**, **back**, and **linings**.

6. With right sides together, sew **front** and 1 **lining** together along top edge. Repeat with **back** and remaining **lining**.

7. Matching right sides, place **front/lining** on top of **back/lining** (Fig. 1); pin. Stitch around clutch, leaving an opening for turning on lining side.

8. Turn clutch right side out through opening. Sew opening closed. Insert lining into clutch.

9. Using pattern, cut 1 yo-yo from *each* of brown and gold fabric scraps. Follow **Making Yo-Yos**, page 61, to make 2 yo-yos. Tack yo-yos to clutch.

10. Sew snap to lining at top edge of clutch.

Design by Linda Lum De Bono

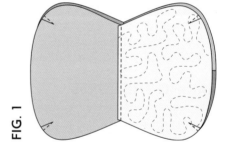

FIG. 1

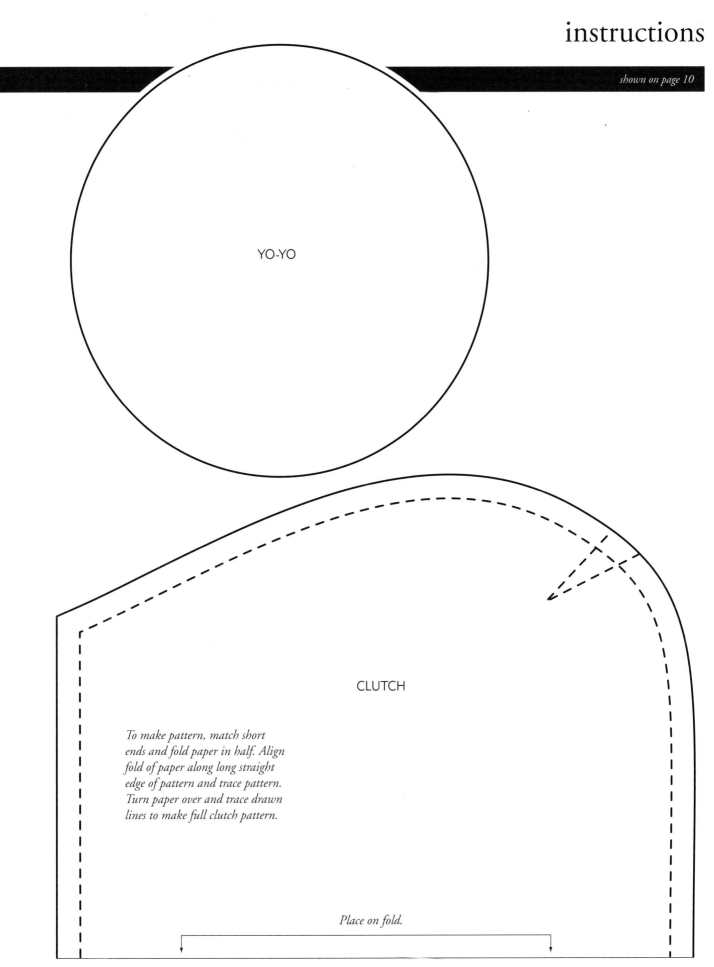

YO-YO

CLUTCH

*To make pattern, match short
ends and fold paper in half. Align
fold of paper along long straight
edge of pattern and trace pattern.
Turn paper over and trace drawn
lines to make full clutch pattern.*

Place on fold.

instructions

SUPPLIES

1 placemat with beads on
short edges (Both sides will
be exposed.)
1 matching tassel
1 yd (91 cm) of $^7/_{32}$" (6 mm)
diameter matching twisted
satin cord
Water- or air-soluble fabric
marking pen

MAKING THE PURSE

1. Matching right sides and short edges, fold placemat in half. Using water- or air-soluble pen, mark "pockets" as shown by pink dashed lines in **Fig. 1**. Stitch through both layers along drawn lines, backstitching at beginning and ending of lines to reinforce.

2. With beads on top, fold placemat in half again. Fold back top and bottom layers and stitch close to side edges of remaining layers as shown in **Fig. 2**.

3. Stitch $^1/_4$" from bottom edge, sewing through all layers (**Fig. 3**).

4. Fold open corner of each "pocket" and tack tassel to 1 pocket. Cut cord to desired length and tie knot in each end. Tack ends to inside of purse.

Design by Linda Tiano

FIG. 1

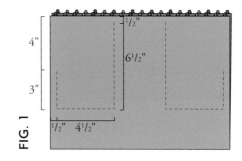

FIG. 2

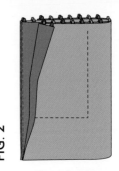

FIG. 3

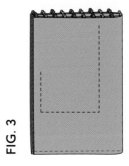

PURSE DIAGRAM

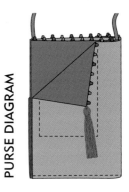

quilt tip

Instead of a tassel, add a charm or a big
wooden bead to the front of your purse.

The pockets on this purse are great for
phones, iPods, make-up, keys....

FINISHED QUILT SIZE:
35½" x 39½" (90 cm x 100 cm)
FINISHED BLOCK SIZE:
10" x 10" (25 cm x 25 cm)

YARDAGE REQUIREMENTS

Yardage is based on 43"/44" (109 cm/112 cm) wide fabric with a "usable width" of 40" (102 cm).

- ½ yd (46 cm) of gold print #1 fabric
- ⅜ yd (34 cm) of gold print #2 fabric
- ¼ yd (23 cm) of lime green print fabric
- ⅜ yd (34 cm) of fuchsia print fabric
- ½ yd (46 cm) of multi-color print fabric for borders
- ⅞ yd (80 cm) of green floral fabric for yo-yos
- 1¼ yds (1.1 m) of fabric for backing
- ⅜ yd (34 cm) of fabric for binding

You will also need:

- 40" x 44" (102 cm x 112 cm) piece of batting
- Letter-size piece of paper for pattern

CUTTING OUT THE PIECES

*Follow **Rotary Cutting**, page 59, to cut fabric. All strips are cut across the width of the fabric. All measurements include ¼" seam allowances.*

From gold print #1 fabric:
- Cut 4 strips 2"w. From these strips, cut 10 **narrow strips** 2" x 10½".
- Cut 2 strips 2½"w. Cut 5 **medium strips** 2½" x 10½".

From gold print #2 fabric:
- Cut 4 strips 3"w. From these strips, cut 10 **wide strips** 3" x 10½".

From lime green print fabric:
- Cut 1 strip 6½"w. From this strip, cut 4 **small squares** 6½" x 6½".

From fuchsia print fabric:
- Cut 4 strips 2½"w. From these strips, cut 8 **large rectangles** 2½" x 10½" and 8 **small rectangles** 2½" x 6½".

From multi-color print fabric:
- Cut 2 **top/bottom borders** 5" x 30½".
- Cut 2 **side borders** 3" x 39½".

From green floral fabric:
- Cut 2 strips 12½"w. From these strips, cut 4 **large squares** 12½" x 12½".

From fabric for binding:
- Cut 5 **binding strips** 2⅛"w.

MAKING THE QUILT TOP

*Follow **Machine Piecing**, page 59, and **Pressing**, page 60. Refer to **Quilt Top Diagram**, page 35, to assemble quilt top. Use ¼" seam allowances throughout.*

1. Sew 2 **narrow strips**, 1 **medium strip**, and 2 **wide strips** together to make **Block A**. Make 5 **Block A's**.
2. Sew 2 **small rectangles** and 1 **small square** together to make **Unit 1**. Make 4 **Unit 1's**.
3. Sew 2 **large rectangles** and 1 **Unit 1** together to make **Block B**. Make 4 **Block B's**.
4. Sew 2 **Block A's** and 1 **Block B** together to make **Row 1**. Make 2 **Row 1's**.
5. Sew 1 **Block A** and 2 **Block B's** together to make **Row 2**.
6. Sew **Rows** together to make quilt top center.
7. Matching centers and corners, sew **top/bottom borders** to quilt top center.
8. Matching centers and corners, sew **side borders** to quilt top center.

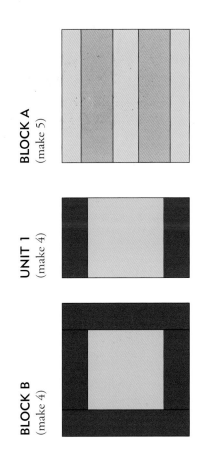

BLOCK A (make 5)

UNIT 1 (make 4)

BLOCK B (make 4)

instructions

COMPLETING THE QUILT

1. Follow **Quilting**, page 61, to mark, layer, and quilt as desired. Our quilt is machine quilted with meander quilting in the blocks and free-form quilting in the borders.

2. Trace $1/4$ yo-yo pattern onto paper; cut out. Fold 1 **large square** in half; fold in half again into a $6^{1}/_{4}$" x $6^{1}/_{4}$" square. Align straight edges of pattern with folds of fabric and cut out along curved edge. Repeat with remaining **large squares**. Follow **Making Yo-Yos**, page 61, to make 4 yo-yos. Tack 1 yo-yo to center of each **Block B**.

3. Follow **Binding for Yo! Quilt**, page 65, to bind quilt.

Design by Linda Lum DeBono

QUILT TOP DIAGRAM

Place on fold.

$1/4$ YO-YO

Place on fold.

instructions

FINISHED PILLOW SIZE:
14" x 14" (36 cm x 36 cm)

YARDAGE REQUIREMENTS

Yardage is based on 43"/44" (109 cm/112 cm) wide fabric with a "usable width" of 40" (102 cm).

$^1/_2$ yd (46 cm) of white solid fabric
$^1/_8$ yd (11 cm) of brown print fabric
$^3/_8$ yd (34 cm) of brown solid fabric
Scraps of solid color fabrics for appliqués (red, hot pink, yellow, green, and yellow-green)
You will also need:
Scrap of purple felt
14" x 14" (36 cm x 36 cm) pillow form
Embroidery floss: yellow-green and turquoise
Rubber alphabet stamp set
Black acrylic paint
Small paintbrush
Stabilizer
Air- or water-soluble fabric marking pen

CUTTING OUT THE PIECES

*Follow **Rotary Cutting**, page 59, to cut fabric. Background square is cut larger than needed and will be trimmed after adding appliqués. All measurements include $^1/_4$" seam allowances (except felt pieces).*

From white solid fabric:
- Cut 1 **background square** 14$^1/_2$" x 14$^1/_2$".

From brown print fabric:
- Cut 2 **side borders** 1$^1/_2$" x 12$^1/_2$".
- Cut 2 **top/bottom borders** 1$^1/_2$" x 14$^1/_2$".

From brown solid fabric:
- Cut 2 **pillow back rectangles** 9$^1/_2$" x 14$^1/_2$".

From purple felt:
- Cut 2 **squares** 1" x 1". Cut squares *once* diagonally to make 4 **triangles**. (You will use 3 and have 1 left over.)

CUTTING OUT THE APPLIQUÉ PIECES

*Follow **Preparing Fusible Appliqué Pieces**, page 60 to cut appliqués using patterns on page 37. Patterns are reversed and do not include seam allowances.*

From scraps of fabrics:
- Cut 3 **hearts** (2 hot pink and 1 red).
- Cut 3 **rectangles** (1 green, 1 yellow, and 1 yellow-green).

MAKING THE PILLOW TOP

*Follow **Machine Piecing**, page 59, and **Pressing** and **Satin Stitch Appliqué**, page 60, to make pillow top. Use $^1/_4$" seam allowances throughout. Refer to **Pillow Diagram** for placement of appliqués and embroidery. **Hand Stitches** are shown on page 66. Use 6 strands of embroidery floss for all embroidery.*

1. Arrange appliqué pieces onto **background square**; fuse in place.
2. Starting and stopping 1$^1/_4$" from edges of **background square**, use a ruler and air- or water-soluble pen to mark straight lines across **background square** for Chain Stitch placement.
3. Paint rubber stamp letters with acrylic paint and stamp "friends" onto **background square**.
4. Using contrasting thread, Satin Stitch appliqué **hearts** and **rectangles** to **background square**.
5. Pin felt **triangles** to **rectangles**. Work Running Stitches to secure **triangles** in place.
6. Work Running Stitch approximately $^1/_4$" inside edges of hearts. Work lines of Chain Stitches on marked lines.
7. Centering design, trim **background square** to 12$^1/_2$" x 12$^1/_2$".
8. Sew **side** and then **top/bottom borders** to **background square** to complete pillow top.

COMPLETING THE PILLOW

1. On each **pillow back rectangle**, press 1 long edge $^1/_4$" to the wrong side; press $^1/_4$" to the wrong side again and stitch in place.
2. Overlap hemmed edges of **pillow back rectangles**, right sides facing up, to form a 14$^1/_2$" x 14$^1/_2$" square for pillow back. Baste **pillow back rectangles** together at overlap.
3. With right sides facing, pin pillow top and pillow back together. Sew around pillow. Remove basting, clip corners, turn, and press. Insert pillow form.

Design by Linda Tiano

PILLOW DIAGRAM

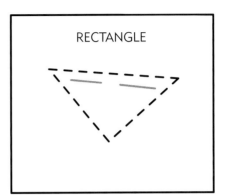

RECTANGLE

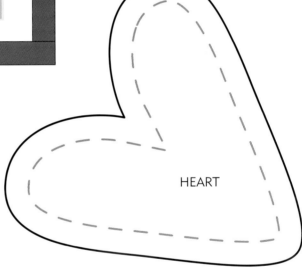

HEART

quilt tips

If you don't want to invest in stamps, embroider your word or words with black embroidery floss or write them with a black permanent pen.

Make your own pillow form using an old shirt and the stuffing from an old pillow.

instructions

FINISHED PILLOW SIZE:
14" x 14" (36 cm x 36 cm)

CUTTING OUT THE PIECES

Follow **Rotary Cutting**, *page 59, to cut fabric. Background square is cut larger than needed and will be trimmed after adding appliqués. All measurements include $1/4$" seam allowances (except felt pieces).*

From white solid fabric:
- Cut 1 **background square** $14^1/2$" x $14^1/2$".

From brown print fabric:
- Cut 2 **side borders** $1^1/2$" x $12^1/2$".
- Cut 2 **top/bottom borders** $1^1/2$" x $14^1/2$".

From brown solid fabric:
- Cut 2 **pillow back rectangles** $9^1/2$" x $14^1/2$".

From yellow-green felt:
- Cut 2 squares $5/8$" x $5/8$". Cut squares *once* diagonally to make 4 **small triangles**. (You will use 3 and have 1 left over.)

CUTTING OUT THE APPLIQUÉ PIECES

Follow **Preparing Fusible Appliqué Pieces**, *page 60, to cut appliqués using patterns on page 39. Patterns are reversed and do not include seam allowances.*

From scraps of fabrics:
- Cut 1 *each* of **large**, **medium**, and **small outer circles** (hot pink).
- Cut 1 *each* of **large**, **medium**, and **small inner circles** (red).
- Cut 1 **large rectangle** (green).
- Cut 1 **small rectangle** (yellow).
- Cut 2 **large triangles** (1 yellow-green and 1 light brown).

YARDAGE REQUIREMENTS

Yardage is based on 43"/44" (109 cm/112 cm) wide fabric with a "usable width" of 40" (102 cm).

$1/2$ yd (46 cm) of white solid fabric
$1/8$ yd (11 cm) of brown print fabric
$3/8$ yd (34 cm) of brown solid fabric
Scraps of solid color fabrics for appliqués (red, hot pink, yellow, green, yellow-green, and light brown)

You will also need:

Scrap of yellow-green felt
14" x 14" (36 cm x 36 cm) pillow form
Embroidery floss: medium green, light green, yellow-green, and turquoise
Rubber alphabet stamp set
Black acrylic paint
Small paintbrush
Stabilizer
Air- or water-soluble fabric marking pen

MAKING THE PILLOW TOP

Follow **Machine Piecing**, *page 59, and* **Pressing** *and* **Satin Stitch Appliqué**, *page 60, to make pillow top. Use $1/4$" seam allowances throughout. Refer to* **Pillow Diagram** *for placement of appliqués and embroidery.* **Hand Stitches** *are shown on page 66. Use 6 strands of embroidery floss for all embroidery.*

1. Arrange appliqué pieces onto **background square**; fuse in place.
2. Stopping $1^1/4$" from edges of **background square**, use a ruler and air- or water-soluble pen to mark straight lines across **background square** for Chain Stitch placement.
3. Paint rubber stamp letters with acrylic paint and stamp "believe" onto **background square**.
4. Using contrasting thread, Satin Stitch appliqué **rectangles**, **circles**, and **large triangles** to **background square**.
5. Pin felt **small triangles** to **inner circles**. Work Straight Stitches to secure **small triangles** in place.
6. Work 5 rows of Running Stitches across **small rectangle**. Work lines of Chain Stitches on marked lines.

7. On each side of "believe," work a large Double Cross Stitch; work a small Cross Stitch in center of each Double Cross Stitch to secure long stitches.
8. Centering design, trim **background square** to $12^1/2$" x $12^1/2$".
9. Sew **side** and then **top/bottom borders** to **background square** to complete pillow top.

COMPLETING THE PILLOW

1. On each **pillow back rectangle**, press 1 long edge $1/4$" to the wrong side; press $1/4$" to the wrong side again and stitch in place.
2. Overlap hemmed edges of **pillow back rectangles**, right sides facing up, to form a $14^1/2$" x $14^1/2$" square for pillow back. Baste **pillow back rectangles** together at overlap.
3. With right sides facing, pin pillow top and pillow back together. Sew around pillow. Remove basting, clip corners, turn, and press. Insert pillow form.

Design by Linda Tiano

PILLOW DIAGRAM

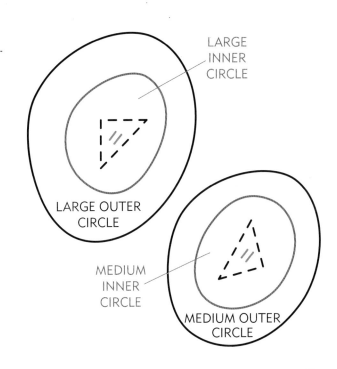

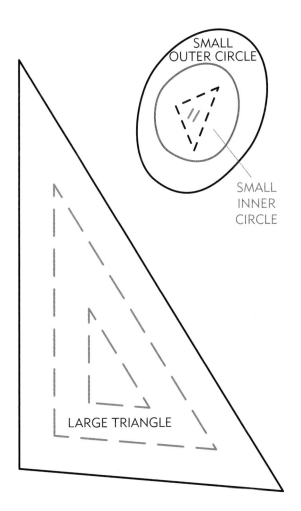

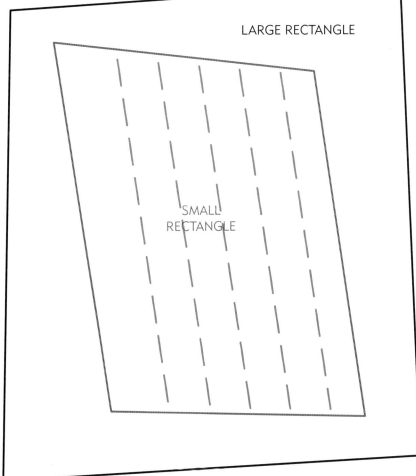

instructions

LOVE PILLOW

FINISHED PILLOW SIZE:
16" x 12" (41 cm x 30 cm)

YARDAGE REQUIREMENTS

Yardage is based on 43"/44" (109 cm/112 cm) wide fabric with a "usable width" of 40" (102 cm).

$1/2$ yd (46 cm) of white solid fabric

$1/8$ yd (11 cm) of brown print fabric

$3/8$ yd (34 cm) of brown solid fabric

Scraps of solid color fabrics for appliqués (hot pink, lime green, yellow-green, red, and pink)

You will also need:

16" x 12" (41 cm x 30 cm) pillow form

Embroidery floss: yellow-green, turquoise, and brown

Rubber alphabet stamp set

Black acrylic paint

Small paintbrush

Stabilizer

Air- or water-soluble fabric marking pen

CUTTING OUT THE PIECES

*Follow **Rotary Cutting**, page 59, to cut fabric. Background rectangle is cut larger than needed and will be trimmed after adding appliqués. All measurements include $1/4$" seam allowances.*

From white solid fabric:
- Cut 1 **background rectangle** $16^1/2$" x $12^1/2$".

From brown print fabric:
- Cut 2 **side borders** $1^1/2$" x $12^1/2$".
- Cut 2 **top/bottom borders** $1^1/2$" x $14^1/2$".

From brown solid fabric:
- Cut 2 **pillow back rectangles** $10^1/2$" x $12^1/2$".

CUTTING OUT THE APPLIQUÉ PIECES

*Follow **Preparing Fusible Appliqué Pieces**, page 60, to cut appliqués using patterns on page 41. Patterns are reversed and do not include seam allowances.*

From scraps of fabrics:
- Cut 1 **heart** (hot pink).
- Cut 1 **large outer circle** (lime green).
- Cut 1 *each* **medium** and **small outer circles** (yellow green).
- Cut 1 *each* **large** and **medium inner circles** (red).
- Cut 1 **small inner circle** (pink).

MAKING THE PILLOW TOP

*Follow **Machine Piecing**, page 59, and **Pressing** and **Satin Stitch Appliqué**, page 60, to make pillow top. Use $1/4$" seam allowances throughout. Refer to **Pillow Diagram** for placement of appliqués and embroidery. **Hand Stitches** are shown on page 66. Use 6 strands of embroidery floss for all embroidery.*

1. Arrange appliqué pieces onto **background rectangle**; fuse in place.
2. Starting and stopping $1^1/4$" from edges of **background rectangle**, use a ruler and air- or water-soluble pen to mark straight lines across **background rectangle** for Chain Stitch placement.
3. Paint rubber stamp letters with acrylic paint and stamp "love you" onto **background rectangle**.
4. Using contrasting thread, Satin Stitch appliqué **heart** and **circles** to **background rectangle**.
5. Work Running Stitch approximately $1/4$" from edges of heart. Work Backstitches and Satin Stitches in center of heart. Work lines of Chain Stitches on marked lines.
6. Centering design, trim **background rectangle** to $14^1/2$" x $10^1/2$".
7. Sew **top/bottom** and then **side borders** to **background rectangle** to complete pillow top.

COMPLETING THE PILLOW

1. On each **pillow back rectangle**, press 1 long edge $1/4$" to the wrong side; press $1/4$" to the wrong side again and stitch in place.
2. Overlap hemmed edges of **pillow back rectangles**, right sides facing up, to form a $16^1/2$" x $12^1/2$" rectangle for pillow back. Baste **pillow back rectangles** together at overlap.
3. With right sides facing, pin pillow top and pillow back together. Sew around pillow. Remove basting, clip corners, turn, and press. Insert pillow form.

Design by Linda Tiano

PILLOW DIAGRAM

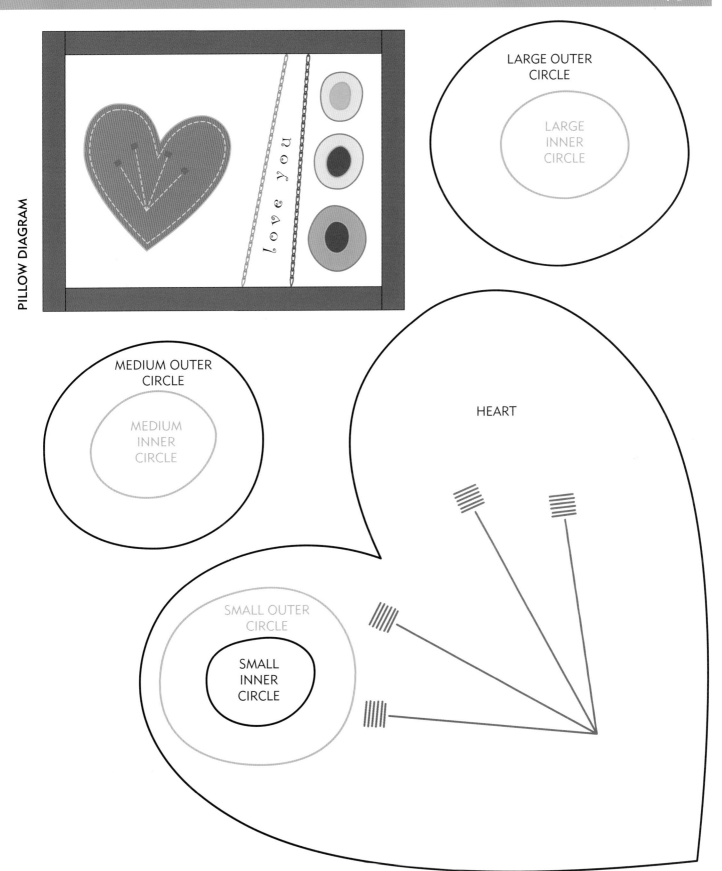

LARGE OUTER
CIRCLE

LARGE
INNER
CIRCLE

MEDIUM OUTER
CIRCLE

MEDIUM
INNER
CIRCLE

HEART

SMALL OUTER
CIRCLE

SMALL
INNER
CIRCLE

love you

instructions

FINISHED QUILT SIZE:
58" x 64" (147 cm x 163 cm)

YARDAGE REQUIREMENTS

Yardage is based on 43"/44" (109 cm/112 cm) wide fabric with a "usable width" of 40" (102 cm).

$1^1/2$ yds (1.4 m) of brown solid fabric
$1^1/8$ yds (1 m) of blue solid fabric
2 yds (1.8 m) of brown/blue polka dot fabric
$^3/4$ yd (69 cm) of brown print fabric (includes binding)
$^7/8$ yd (80 cm) of white solid fabric
$3^7/8$ yds (3.5 m) of fabric for backing

You will also need:

62" x 68" (157 cm x 173 cm) piece of batting
1 yd (91 cm) of 22" (56 cm) wide woven interfacing
Tracing paper
505® temporary fabric spray adhesive
Embroidery floss: pink, blue, and brown
Water- or air-soluble fabric marking pen

CUTTING OUT THE PIECES

Follow **Rotary Cutting,** *page 59, to cut fabric. Background square is cut larger than needed and will be trimmed after adding appliqués. All measurements include $^1/4$" seam allowances.*

From brown solid fabric:

- Cut 2 strips $15^3/4$"w. From these strips, cut 1 *each* of rectangles **#1, #3, #7,** and **#9** $15^3/4$" x $17^3/4$".
- Cut 1 **rectangle #5** 17" x 19".

From blue solid fabric:

- Cut 1 strip 17"w. From this strip, cut 1 *each* of rectangles **#2** and **#8** 17" x $17^3/4$".
- Cut 1 strip $15^3/4$"w. From this strip, cut 1 *each* of rectangles **#4** and **#6** $15^3/4$" x 19".

From brown/blue polka dot fabric:

- Cut 2 *lengthwise* **side borders** $5^1/4$" x 64".
- Cut 2 *lengthwise* **top/bottom borders** $5^1/4$" x $48^1/2$".
- Cut 2 *lengthwise* **horizontal sashings** 4" x $48^1/2$".
- Cut 2 *lengthwise* **vertical sashings** 4" x $54^1/2$".

From brown print fabric:

- Cut 7 **binding strips** 2"w.
- Cut 1 strip $10^1/2$"w. From this strip, cut 4 **appliqué rectangles** $8^1/2$" x $10^1/2$".

CUTTING OUT THE APPLIQUÉ PIECES

Trace patterns on pages 45 – 46 onto tracing paper and cut out. Use tracing paper patterns to cut the following appliqué pieces.

From white solid fabric:

- Cut 2 **leaves** and 2 **leaves in reverse.**
- Cut 2 **stems** and 2 **stems in reverse.**
- Cut 10 **large circles** (for petals).

From woven interfacing:

- Cut 2 **leaves.**
- Cut 2 **stems.**
- Cut 6 **large circles.**
- Cut 1 **small circle.**

From blue solid fabric:

- Cut 2 **large circles** (for flower center).

From brown print fabric:

- Cut 2 **small circles** (for flower center).

PIECING THE QUILT

Follow **Machine Piecing,** *page 59, and* **Pressing,** *page 60, to make quilt top. Use $^1/4$" seam allowances except where noted otherwise.*

1. Follow Steps 2 – 3 of **Preparing the Backing,** page 62, to make a 62" x 68" backing.

2. Layer backing, wrong side up, and batting. Fold back half of batting and spray the wrong side of the backing with adhesive. Smooth batting over backing and repeat for other half. Turn backing and batting over and smooth out backing. With batting side up, use water- or air-soluble pen to mark lines 7" from top and left edges.

quilt tip

Linda spread a sheet out on the floor before layering the backing and batting. The sheet protected her carpet from the spray adhesive.

3. Spray batting with adhesive. Aligning **rectangles** along drawn lines and placing edges together, arrange **rectangles #1 – #9** on batting as shown in **Fig. 1**.

4. Press long edges of **sashings** ¹⁄₂" to wrong side.

5. With right sides together, fold **sashings** in half lengthwise; finger press. Align fold of 1 **vertical sashing** with edges of **rectangles** between left and center columns (**Fig. 2**). Unfold sashing, smooth, and pin in place. Sewing though all layers, topstitch approximately ¹⁄₁₆" from long edges of **vertical sashing**. Repeat to sew remaining **vertical sashing** between center and right columns.

6. In the same manner, sew 2 **horizontal sashings** between rows.

7. Matching right sides and raw edges and sewing through all layers, sew **top border** to top edge of quilt top (**rectangles #1 – #3**). Repeat to sew **bottom** and then **side borders** to quilt top.

8. To stabilize quilt, machine baste around quilt ¹⁄₈" from edges of quilt top.

ADDING THE APPLIQUÉS AND EMBROIDERY

*Refer to **Quilt Diagram** for placement of appliqués and embroidery. **Hand Stitches** are shown on page 66. Use 6 strands of embroidery floss for all embroidery.*

1. Layer 1 **leaf in reverse** (right side up), 1 **leaf** (right side down), and **leaf** interfacing. Sew around edges. Clip seam allowances or trim close to stitching with pinking shears. Cut a slit in center of back of leaf, turn right side out, and press. Repeat to make 2nd leaf and 2 stems. Work brown Running Stitches around edges of leaves and down center of stems.

FIG. 1

FIG. 2

2. In the same manner, make 5 petals and 1 *each* of large and small flower centers. Work pink and blue Running Stitches on petals and blue Running Stitches on large flower center.

3. Press all edges of 4 **appliqué rectangles** ¹⁄₄" to wrong side.

4. Pin appliqués to quilt top and topstitch each to quilt top approximately ¹⁄₁₆" from edges of appliqués using matching thread and sewing through all layers.

COMPLETING THE QUILT

1. Follow **Types of Quilting Designs**, page 61, and **Marking Quilting Lines**, page 62, and **Machine Quilting Methods**, page 63, to add additional quilting as desired. Linda used the leaf pattern to quilt a leaf in **rectangles #1** and **#9**. She meander quilted in the backgrounds around the quilted and appliquéd leaves.

2. Follow **Binding for Where's Everybody Going? Quilt**, page 65, to bind quilt.

Design by Linda Tiano

QUILT DIAGRAM

Black or blue solid lines represent cutting lines. Dashed lines represent stitching lines. Gray solid lines indicate embroidery details.

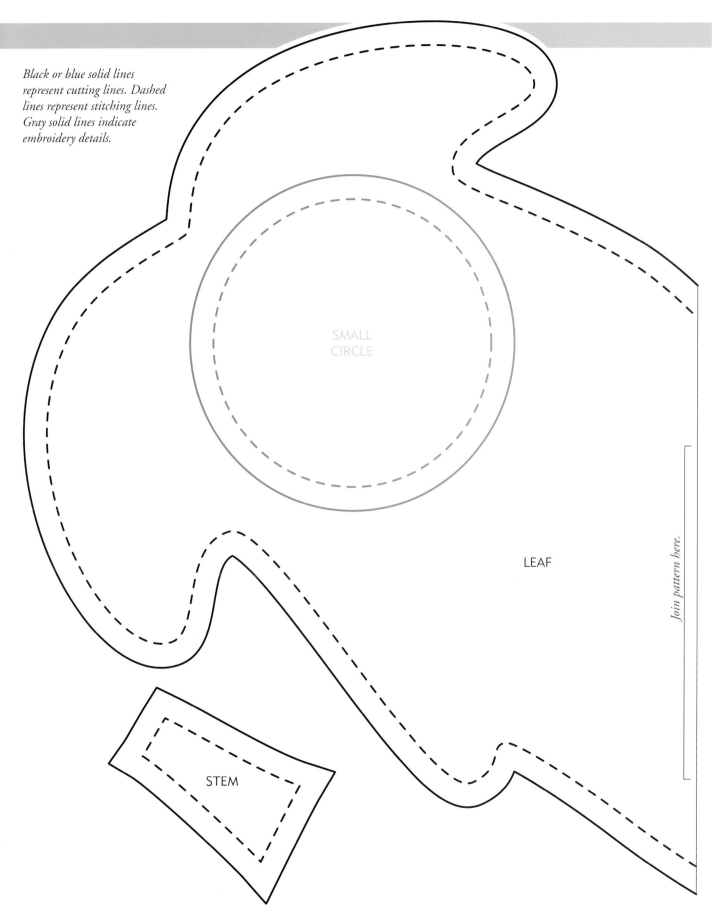

SMALL CIRCLE

LEAF

STEM

Join pattern here.

instructions

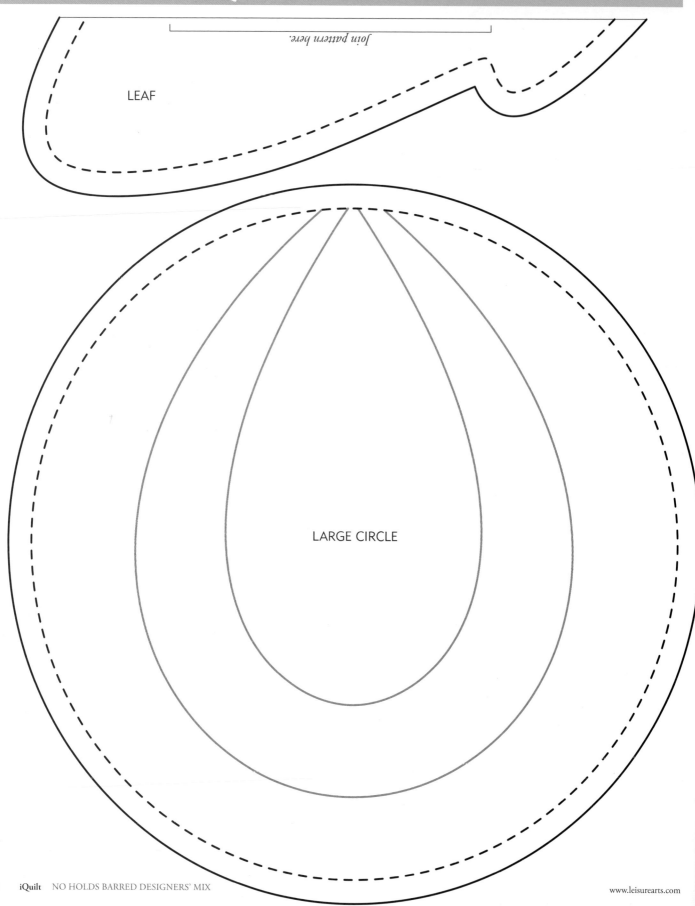

LEAF

Join pattern here.

LARGE CIRCLE

MADE YOU LOOK FRAMED QUILT

shown on page 17

FRAME OPENING SIZE:
13" x 19" (33 cm x 48 cm). *Size of frame opening may vary within a few inches each direction.*

YARDAGE REQUIREMENTS

Yardage is based on 43"/44" (109 cm/112 cm) wide fabric with a "usable width" of 40" (102 cm).

Fat quarter* *each* of orange print, green stripe, brown polka dot, and brown print fabrics

Scrap *each* of brown floral and blue print fabric

You will also need:

$18^1/2$" x $24^1/2$" (47 cm x 62 cm) piece of batting

13" x 19" (33 cm x 48 cm) piece of foam core board *(or size of frame opening)*

Paper-backed fusible web

Hot glue gun or staple gun

Stabilizer

*Fat quarter = 18" x 20" (46 cm x 51 cm)

CUTTING OUT THE PIECES

*Follow **Rotary Cutting**, page 59, to cut fabric. All measurements include $^1/4$" seam allowances.*

From orange print fabric:
- Cut 1 **large rectangle** 13" x 19".

From brown polka dot fabric:
- Cut 1 **medium rectangle** 6" x 19".

From brown print fabric:
- Cut 1 **small rectangle** 6" x $18^1/2$".

CUTTING OUT THE APPLIQUÉ PIECES

*Follow **Preparing Fusible Appliqué Pieces**, page 60, to cut appliqués using patterns on pages 48 – 49. Patterns are reversed and do not include seam allowances.*

From green stripe fat quarter:
- Cut 1 **stem**.

From brown floral scrap:
- Cut 1 **flower**.

From blue print scrap:
- Cut 1 **flower center**.

MAKING THE FRAMED QUILT

*Follow **Machine Piecing**, page 59, **Pressing** and **Satin Stitch Appliqué**, page 60, to make quilt top. Use $^1/4$" seam allowances throughout. Refer to **Quilt Top Diagram** for placement of appliqués.*

1. Arrange appliqué pieces onto **large rectangle** $1^1/2$" from right edge and $2^1/2$" from bottom edge of rectangle; fuse in place. Using matching thread, Satin Stitch appliqué each appliqué piece to rectangle.

2. Sew **large rectangle** and **medium rectangle** together, and then sew **small rectangle** to bottom edge to make quilt top.

3. Layer batting and quilt top (right side up). Follow **Quilting**, page 61, to baste layers together and quilt in the ditch between rectangles and around appliquéd design.

4. Stretch quilt top over foam core board and hot glue or staple edges on back. Secure inside frame.

Design by Linda Lum DeBono

QUILT TOP DIAGRAM

instructions

STEM

FLOWER
CENTER

FLOWER

12 1/2 = 1/4" seams
+ 1/4
12 3/4 cut size to get 1/2" seams

Blocks - cut 12 3/4"
nud 9
center is one of a kind
other 8 = 2 similar or exact
x 4

instructions

BLOOMING BABY QUILT

FINISHED QUILT SIZE:
46³/₄" x 46³/₄" (119 cm x 119 cm)
FINISHED BLOCK SIZE:
12" x 12" (30 cm x 30 cm)

CUTTING OUT THE PIECES

Follow Rotary Cutting, page 59, to cut fabric. All strips are cut across the width of the fabric. All measurements include ¹/₄" seam allowances.

From turquoise stripe fabric:
• Cut 4 **inner border strips** 1¹/₂"w.
From orange print fabric:
• Cut 5 **outer border strips** 4¹/₂"w.
From binding fabric:
• Cut 6 **binding strips** 2¹/₈"w.

MAKING THE QUILT TOP

Follow Machine Piecing, page 59, and Pressing, page 60. Refer to Quilt Top Diagram to assemble quilt top. Use ¹/₄" seam allowances throughout.

1. Sew **Blocks** together in 3 **Rows** of 3 **Blocks** to make quilt top center.
2. To determine length of **side inner borders**, measure *length* of quilt top center. From **inner border strips**, cut 2 **side inner borders** the determined length. Matching centers and corners, scw **side inner borders** to quilt top center.

YARDAGE REQUIREMENTS

Yardage is based on 43"/44" (109 cm/112 cm) wide fabric with a "usable width" of 40" (102 cm).
— 12¹/₂" x 12¹/₂" (32 cm x 32 cm) square *each* of 9 coordinating fabrics
¹/₄ yd (23 cm) of turquoise stripe fabric
³/₄ yd (69 cm) of orange print fabric
2⁷/₈ yds (2.6 m) of backing fabric
¹/₂ yd (46 cm) of binding fabric
You will also need:
51" x 51" (130 cm x 130 cm) piece of batting

3. To determine length of **top/bottom inner borders**, measure *width* of quilt top center (including added borders). From **remaining inner border strips**, cut 2 **top/bottom inner borders** the determined length. Matching centers and corners, sew **top/bottom inner borders** to quilt top center.

4. To determine length of **side outer borders**, measure *length* of quilt top. From outer border strips, cut 2 **outer side borders** the determined length. Matching centers and corners, sew **side outer borders** to quilt top.

5. Sew remaining **outer border strips** together end to end.

6. To determine length of **top/bottom outer borders**, measure *width* of quilt top (including added borders). From remaining **outer border strips**, cut 2 **outer top/bottom borders** the determined length. Matching centers and corners, sew **top/bottom outer borders** to quilt top.

COMPLETING THE QUILT

1. Follow **Quilting**, page 61, to mark, layer, and quilt as desired. Our quilt is machine quilted. The inner border and squares are quilted in the ditch. An "X" is quilted (corner to corner) in center and corner squares. A 6" x 6" square is quilted in the remaining squares.

2. Follow **Binding for Blooming Baby Quilt**, page 64, to bind quilt.

Design by L.A. Staff

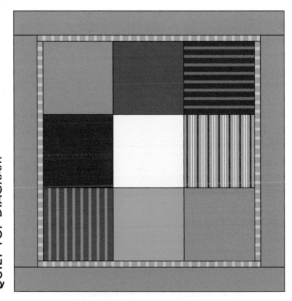

QUILT TOP DIAGRAM

Baby Bloom collection pattern tested by Nelwyn Gray and Lانwie Barnett

instructions

FINISHED SKIRT SIZE:
52" x 27" x 16" (132 cm x 69 cm x 41 cm)

CUTTING OUT THE PIECES

*Follow **Rotary Cutting**, page 59, to cut fabric. All strips are cut across the width of the fabric. All measurements include $^1/_2$" seam allowances.*

From muslin:
- Cut 1 **decking** 53" x 28".

From turquoise print fabric:
- Cut 4 *crosswise* **front/back panels** $39^3/_4$" x $13^1/_2$".
- Cut 2 *crosswise* **side panels** $36^1/_2$ x $13^1/_2$".

From brown print fabric:
- Cut 4 *crosswise* **front/back borders** $39^3/_4$" x 8".
- Cut 2 *crosswise* **side borders** $36^1/_2$" x 8".

YARDAGE REQUIREMENTS

Yardage is based on 43"/44" (109 cm/112 cm) wide fabric with a "usable width" of 40" (102 cm).

$1^5/_8$ yds (1.5 m) of muslin for decking
$2^1/_2$ yds (2.3 m) of turquoise print fabric
$1^1/_2$ yds (1.4 m) of brown print fabric

MAKING THE CRIB SKIRT

Use $^1/_2$" seam allowances throughout.

1. Sew 2 turquoise print **front/back panels** together end to end to make **skirt front**.
2. Press 1 short end of **skirt front** $^1/_4$" to wrong side; press $^1/_4$" to wrong side again. Stitch hem in place along fold. Repeat for remaining short side.
3. Sew 2 **front/back borders** together end to end to make **front border**.
4. Press 1 short end of **front border** $^1/_4$" to wrong side; press $^1/_4$" to wrong side again. Stitch hem in place along fold. Repeat for remaining short side.
5. Matching wrong sides, press **front border** in half lengthwise. Baste raw edges together.
6. Matching right sides and raw edges, sew **front border** to **skirt front**. Press seam allowances toward **skirt front**.
7. Fold and press pleats as shown in **Fig. 1**; baste pleats across top edge.
8. Repeat Steps 1 – 7 for **skirt back**.
9. Repeat Steps 1 – 7 using 1 **side panel** and 1 **side border** for each **skirt side** and folding and pressing pleats as shown in **Fig. 2**.
10. Beginning and ending $^1/_2$" from corners of decking and matching right sides and raw edges, sew skirts to **decking**. Press seam allowances toward **decking**.

Design by L. A. Stuff

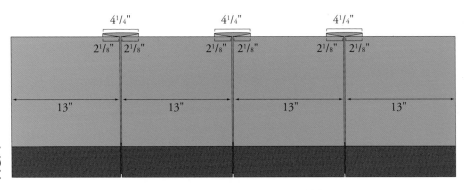

FIG. 1

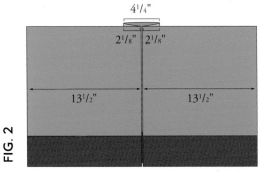

FIG. 2

MAMA'S NEW BAG

FINISHED BAG SIZE:
17¹/₂" x 14³/₄" (44 cm x 37 cm)

CUTTING OUT THE PIECES

*Follow **Rotary Cutting**, page 59, to cut fabric. All measurements include ¹/₂" seam allowances.*

From orange print fabric:
- Cut 2 **bag front/backs** 18" x 15".
- Cut 2 **ties** 2¹/₂" x 32".

From turquoise stripe fabric:
- Cut 1 **pocket** 11³/₄" x 9".

From red print fabric:
- Cut 2 **bag linings** 18" x 16".
- Cut 1 **pocket lining** 11³/₄" x 9".
- Cut 1 **pocket binding strip** 1" x 11³/₄".

From batting:
- Cut 2 **bag battings** 18" x 15".
- Cut 1 **pocket batting** 11³/₄" x 9".

MAKING THE TOY BAG

*Follow **Machine Piecing**, page 59, and **Pressing**, page 60. Use ¹/₄" seam allowances throughout.*

1. Using a plate approximately 10" in diameter as pattern, round bottom corners of **bag front/backs**, **bag linings**, and **bag battings** (**Fig. 1**).

2. Using a plate approximately 6¹/₄" in diameter as pattern, round bottom corners of **pocket**, **pocket lining**, and **pocket batting**.

YARDAGE REQUIREMENTS

Yardage is based on 43"/44" (109 cm/112 cm) wide fabric with a "usable width" of 40" (102 cm).
- ⁵/₈ yd (57 cm) of orange print fabric
- ³/₈ yd (34 cm) of turquoise stripe fabric
- ⁷/₈ yd (80 cm) of red print fabric

You will also need:
- 34" x 31" (86 cm x 79 cm) piece of batting

3. Layer **pocket** (right side up), **pocket lining** (wrong side up), and **pocket batting**. Stitch around edges, leaving opening on top edge for turning. Clip corners, turn right side out, and press.

4. Press all edges of **pocket binding strip** ¹/₄" to wrong side. Matching wrong sides, press **pocket binding strip** in half *lengthwise*. Place folded **strip** over top edge of **pocket** and stitch near bottom edge of strip through all layers.

5. Layer 1 **bag batting** and **bag front** (right side up) and pin together. Center and pin **pocket** on **bag front**. Stitching through all layers, sew side and bottom edges of **pocket** to **bag front** (**Fig. 2**).

6. Layer **bag front** (right side up), **bag back** (right side down), and remaining **bag batting**. Stitch side and bottom edges together. Clip curves as needed, and turn right side out.

7. With right sides together, sew **bag linings** together along side and bottom edges. Press top edge of lining ¹/₂" to wrong side.

8. Place lining inside bag. Fold top edge of lining ¹/₂" over top edge of bag and stitch in place.

9. For each **tie**, fold tie in half *lengthwise*. Stitch raw edges together, leaving an opening for turning. Clip corners and turn right side out; stitch opening closed.

10. Matching short ends, fold **ties** in half. Stitch folded end of **ties** along binding seam inside of bag at side seams.

FIG. 1

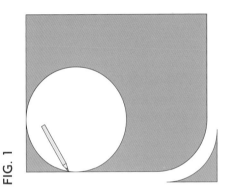

FIG. 2

Design by L.A. Staff

instructions

CRIB SIZE: 27" x 52" (69 cm x 132 cm)

YARDAGE REQUIREMENTS

Yardage is based on 43"/44" (109 cm/112 cm) wide fabric with a "usable width" of 40" (102 cm).

> $5^3/8$ yds (4.9 m) of orange print fabric
> $5^3/8$ yds (4.9 m) of muslin

You will also need:

> Fairfield Nu-Foam® Bumper Pad Set
> $4^1/8$ yds (3.8 m) Velcro® brand hook and loop fastener
> Polyester fiberfill

CUTTING OUT THE PIECES

*Follow **Rotary Cutting**, page 59, to cut fabric. All measurements include $^1/2$" seam allowances.*

From orange print fabric:

- Cut 12 **rectangles** $14^1/2$" x 30".
- Cut 24 **ties** 2" x 20".

From muslin:

- Cut 12 **rectangles** $14^1/2$" x 30".

MAKING THE QUILT TOP

*Follow **Machine Piecing**, page 59, and **Pressing**, page 60. Use $^1/2$" seam allowances throughout.*

1. For each **tie**, press all edges of **tie** $^1/4$" to wrong side. Fold in half lengthwise with wrong sides together and stitch around edges.

2. Matching short ends, fold **ties** in half. Referring to **Fig. 1**, baste folded ends of 4 **ties** to each of 6 orange print **rectangles**. Pin loose ends of **ties** away from seamlines so they do not get caught when stitching.

3. With right sides facing, pin 1 orange print **rectangle** with ties and 1 orange print **rectangle** without ties together. Stitch around edges, leaving 24" opening in center of 1 long edge for fastener. Clip corners and turn right side out.

4. Cut six 24" lengths of fastener. Sew hook side of fastener along 1 side of opening and loop side along remaining side of opening as shown in **Fig. 2**.

5. For each pillow form, pin 2 muslin **rectangles** together along raw edges. Stitch around all sides, leaving an opening along bottom edge for turning. Turn right side out.

6. Insert 1 piece of Nu-Foam® in each pillow form. Stuff pillow form with fiberfill on each side of Nu-Foam® until form is plump. Stitch opening closed.

7. Insert 1 pillow form into each bumper cover.

Design by L.A. Staff

FIG. 1

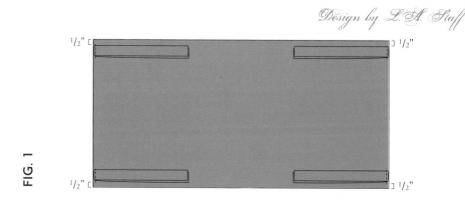

FIG. 2

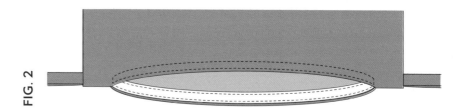

THE TORTOISE AND THE HARE TOYS

shown on page 23

YARDAGE REQUIREMENTS

Yardage is based on 43"/44" (109 cm/112 cm) wide fabric with a "usable width" of 40" (102 cm).

$1/4$ yd (23 cm) of turquoise stripe fabric

$1/4$ yd (23 cm) of orange print fabric

Scraps of cream print and turquoise print fabrics

You will also need:

Polyester fiberfill

Water- or air-soluble fabric marking pen

Brown #5 pearl cotton

Copy or tracing paper

FINISHED HARE SIZE:
Approximately $9^1/_2$" (24 cm) tall
FINISHED TORTOISE SIZE:
Approximately 6" (15 cm) tall

CUTTING OUT THE PIECES

Patterns for toys are on pages 57 – 58. Trace patterns onto paper. Solid black lines indicate cutting, dashed black lines indicate stitching, and gray solid lines indicate embroidery.

From turquoise stripe fabric:
- Cut 1 **hare body** and 1 **hare body in reverse**.
- Cut 1 **hare ear** and 1 **hear ear in reverse**.

From orange print fabric:
- Cut 1 **tortoise body** and 1 **tortoise body in reverse**.

From cream print fabric:
- Cut 1 **hare ear** and 1 **hare ear in reverse**.

From turquoise print fabric:
- Cut 1 **tortoise head** and 1 **tortoise head in reverse**.
- Cut 2 **tortoise feet** and 2 **tortoise feet in reverse**.
- Cut 1 **tortoise tail** and 1 **tortoise tail in reverse**.

MAKING THE TOYS

*Follow **Machine Piecing**, page 59, and **Pressing**, page 60. Use $1/4$" seam allowances throughout. Hand Stitches are on page 66.*

HARE

1. With right sides together, scw 1 turquoise **ear** to 1 cream **ear**, leaving straight edge open for turning. Clip curves and turn ear right side out. Repeat for second ear.

2. Pin a small tuck on straight edge of each ear. Matching raw edges, pin folded edge of cream side of ears to right side of **hare body**. With right sides together, pin **hare body** and **hare body in reverse** together. Sew around edges, catching ears and leaving an opening for turning along bottom edge.

3. Clip curves and turn hare right side out. Fill with fiberfill and stitch opening closed.

4. Using water- or air-soluble pen, draw face using pattern as a suggestion. Using brown pearl cotton, Satin Stitch eyes and nose and Backstitch mouth and whiskers.

TORTOISE

1. With right sides together, sew **head** to **head in reverse**, leaving straight edge open for turning. Clip curves and turn head right side out. Lightly fill with fiberfill.

2. With right sides together, sew 1 **foot** to 1 **foot in reverse**, leaving straight edge open for turning. Clip corners and turn foot right side out. Repeat for second foot and tail.

3. Matching raw edges, pin head, feet, and tail to right side of **tortoise body**. With right sides together, pin **tortoise body** and **tortoise body in reverse** together. Sew around edges, catching head, feet, and tail, and leaving an opening for turning along bottom edge between feet.

4. Clip curves and turn tortoise right side out. Fill with fiberfill and stitch opening closed.

5. Using water- or air-soluble pen, draw face and toes using patterns as a suggestion. Using brown pearl cotton, Satin Stitch eye and nostril and Backstitch mouth and toes.

Design by L. A. Staff

instructions

YARDAGE REQUIREMENTS

Yardage is based on 43"/44" (109 cm/112 cm) wide fabric with a "usable width" of 40" (102 cm).

⅝ yd (57 cm) of turquoise stripe fabric

Scraps of brown print, brown stripe, red print, and red stripe fabrics

You will also need:

Two 14" x 14" (36 cm x 36 cm) artist canvases

Paper-backed fusible web

Black permanent fabric marking pen

Hot glue gun *or* staple gun

FINISHED SIZE:

14" x 14" (36 cm x 36 cm) *each*

CUTTING OUT THE PIECES

Follow **Rotary Cutting**, *page 59, to cut backgrounds. Follow* **Preparing Fusible Appliqués**, *page 60, to cut tortoise and hare using patterns on pages 56 – 58.*

From turquoise stripe fabric:

- Cut 2 background squares 19" x 19".

From brown print fabric:

- Cut 1 **hare body.**
- Cut 1 **left outer ear.**
- Cut 1 **right outer ear.**

From red stripe fabric:

- Cut 1 **left inner ear.**
- Cut 1 **right inner ear.**

From red print fabric:

- Cut 1 **tortoise body.**

From brown stripe fabric:

- Cut 1 **tortoise head.**
- Cut 2 **tortoise feet.**
- Cut 1 **tortoise tail.**

MAKING THE WALL ART

1. Stretch 1 **background square** over canvas and hot glue or staple edges on back.

2. Using black permanent pen, draw details onto tortoise and hare, using gray lines on patterns as a suggestion.

3. Arrange appliqué pieces onto canvases. Fuse appliqués in place.

Design by L.A. Staff

The patterns on this page are for wall art, are reversed, and do not include seam allowances. Gray solid lines indicate ink details. Black dotted lines indicate overlap.

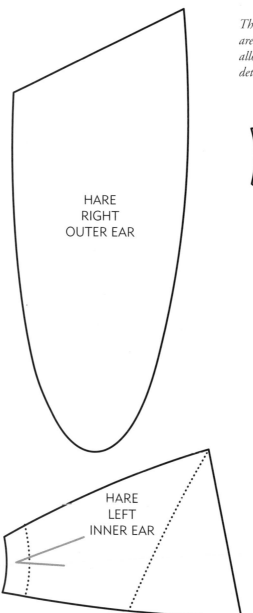

HARE
RIGHT
OUTER EAR

HARE
RIGHT
INNER EAR

HARE
LEFT
OUTER EAR

HARE
LEFT
INNER EAR

THE TORTOISE AND THE HARE

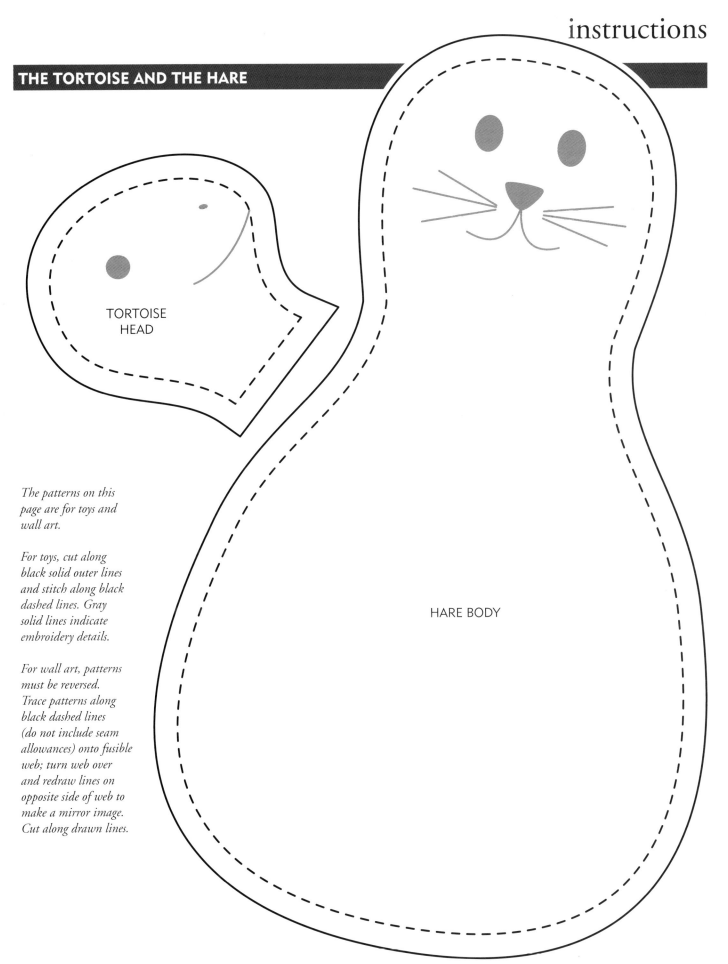

TORTOISE
HEAD

The patterns on this
page are for toys and
wall art.

For toys, cut along
black solid outer lines
and stitch along black
dashed lines. Gray
solid lines indicate
embroidery details.

For wall art, patterns
must be reversed.
Trace patterns along
black dashed lines
(do not include seam
allowances) onto fusible
web; turn web over
and redraw lines on
opposite side of web to
make a mirror image.
Cut along drawn lines.

HARE BODY

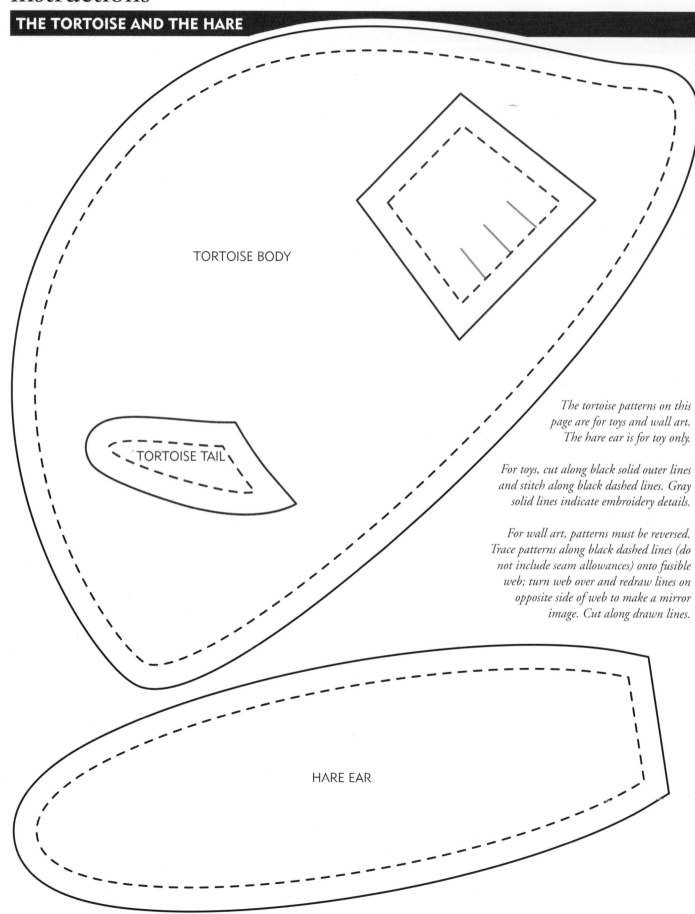

TORTOISE BODY

TORTOISE TAIL

The tortoise patterns on this page are for toys and wall art. The hare ear is for toy only.

For toys, cut along black solid outer lines and stitch along black dashed lines. Gray solid lines indicate embroidery details.

For wall art, patterns must be reversed. Trace patterns along black dashed lines (do not include seam allowances) onto fusible web; turn web over and redraw lines on opposite side of web to make a mirror image. Cut along drawn lines.

HARE EAR

general instructions

To make your quilting easier and more enjoyable, we encourage you to carefully read all of the general instructions, study the color photographs, and familiarize yourself with the individual project instructions before beginning a project.

FABRICS

SELECTING FABRICS

Choose high-quality, medium-weight 100% cotton fabrics. All-cotton fabrics hold a crease better, fray less, and are easier to quilt than cotton/polyester blends.

Yardage requirements listed for each project are based on 43"/44" wide fabric with a "usable" width of 40" after shrinkage and trimming selvages. Actual usable width will probably vary slightly from fabric to fabric. Our recommended yardage lengths should be adequate for occasional re-squaring of fabric when many cuts are required.

PREPARING FABRICS

We recommend that all fabrics be washed, dried, and pressed before cutting. If fabrics are not pre-washed, washing the finished project will cause shrinkage. Bright and dark colors, which may run, should always be washed before cutting. After washing and drying fabric, fold lengthwise with wrong sides together and matching selvages.

ROTARY CUTTING

Rotary cutting has brought speed and accuracy to quiltmaking by allowing quilters to easily cut strips of fabric and then cut those strips into smaller pieces.

- Place fabric on work surface with fold closest to you.

- Cut all strips from the selvage-to-selvage width of the fabric unless otherwise indicated in project instructions.

- Square left edge of fabric using rotary cutter and rulers (**Figs. 1 – 2**).

- To cut each strip required for a project, place ruler over cut edge of fabric, aligning desired marking on ruler with cut edge; make cut (**Fig. 3**).

- When cutting several strips from a single piece of fabric, it is important to make sure that cuts remain at a perfect right angle to the fold; square fabric as needed.

FIG. 1

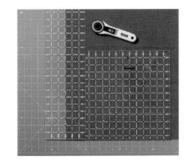

FIG. 2

FIG. 3

MACHINE PIECING

Precise cutting, followed by accurate piecing, will ensure that all pieces of quilt top fit together well.

- Set sewing machine stitch length for approximately 11 stitches per inch.

- Use neutral-colored general-purpose sewing thread (not quilting thread) in needle and in bobbin.

- An accurate $1/4$" seam allowance is *essential*. Presser feet that are $1/4$" wide are available for most sewing machines.

- When piecing, always place pieces right sides together and match raw edges; pin if necessary.

- Chain piecing saves time and will usually result in more accurate piecing.

- Trim away points of seam allowances that extend beyond edges of sewn pieces.

SEWING ACROSS SEAM INTERSECTIONS

When sewing across intersection of two seams, place pieces right sides together and match seams exactly, making sure seam allowances are pressed in opposite directions (**Fig. 4**).

FIG. 4

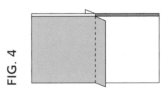

general instructions

PRESSING

- Use steam iron set on "Cotton" for all pressing.

- Press after sewing each seam.

- Seam allowances are almost always pressed to one side, usually toward darker fabric. However, to reduce bulk it may occasionally be necessary to press seam allowances toward the lighter fabric or even to press them open.

- To prevent dark fabric seam allowance from showing through light fabric, trim darker seam allowance slightly narrower than lighter seam allowance.

- To press long seams without curving or other distortion, lay fabric across width of the ironing board.

PREPARING FUSIBLE APPLIQUÉ PIECES

White or light-colored fabrics may need to be lined with fusible interfacing before applying fusible web to prevent darker fabrics from showing through.

1. Place paper-backed fusible web, paper side up, over appliqué pattern. Trace pattern onto paper side of web with pencil as many times as indicated in project instructions for a single fabric.

2. Follow manufacturer's instructions to fuse traced patterns to wrong side of fabrics. Do not remove paper backing.

3. Use scissors to cut out appliqué pieces along traced line. Remove paper backing from all pieces.

SATIN STITCH APPLIQUÉ

A good satin stitch is a thick, smooth, almost solid line of zigzag stitching that covers the exposed raw edges of appliqué pieces.

1. Pin stabilizer, such as paper or any of the commercially available products, on wrong side of background fabric before stitching appliqués in place.

2. Thread sewing machine with general-purpose thread; use general-purpose thread that matches background fabric in bobbin.

3. Set sewing machine for a medium (approximately $1/8$") zigzag stitch and a short stitch length for a more solid line, as used on the pillows, pages 36 – 41. Use a slightly longer stitch for a looser zigzag, as used on *Made You Look Framed Quilt*, page 47. Slightly loosening the top tension may yield a smoother stitch.

4. Begin by stitching two or three stitches in place (drop feed dogs or set stitch length at 0) to anchor thread. Most of the Satin Stitch should be on the appliqué with the right edge of the stitch falling at the outside edge of the appliqué. Stitch over all exposed raw edges of appliqué pieces.

5. (***Note:*** Dots on **Figs. 5 – 10** indicate where to leave needle in fabric when pivoting.) For outside corners, stitch just past corner, stopping with needle in background fabric (**Fig. 5**). Raise presser foot. Pivot project, lower presser foot, and stitch adjacent side (**Fig. 6**).

6. For inside corners, stitch just past corner, stopping with needle in appliqué fabric (**Fig. 7**). Raise presser foot. Pivot project, lower presser foot, and stitch adjacent side (**Fig. 8**).

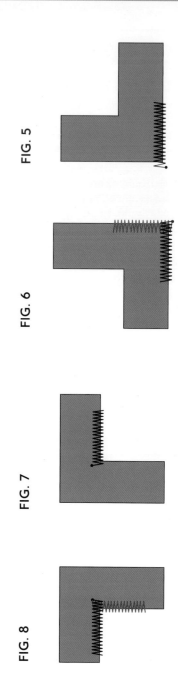

FIG. 5

FIG. 6

FIG. 7

FIG. 8

7. When stitching outside curves, stop with needle in background fabric. Raise presser foot and pivot project as needed. Lower presser foot and continue stitching, pivoting as often as necessary to follow curve (**Fig. 9**).

8. When stitching inside curves, stop with needle in appliqué fabric. Raise presser foot and pivot project as needed. Lower presser foot and continue stitching, pivoting as often as necessary to follow curve (**Fig. 10**).

9. Do not backstitch at end of stitching. Pull threads to wrong side of background fabric; knot thread and trim ends.

10. Carefully tear away stabilizer.

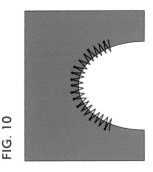

FIG. 10

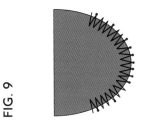

FIG. 9

MAKING YO-YOS

1. Cut the size and number of yo-yos called for in project instructions.

2. Turn edge of yo-yo ¹/₄" to wrong side and make a Running Stitch (page 66) around edge using 2 strands of thread (**Fig. 11**). Pull threads tight from both ends and tie a knot; clip threads (**Fig. 12**)

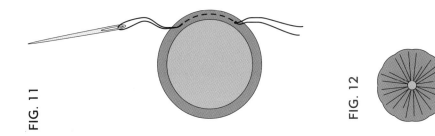

FIG. 11   FIG. 12

QUILTING

*Quilting holds the three layers (top, batting, and backing) of the quilt together and can be done by hand or machine. Because marking, layering, and quilting are interrelated and may be done in different orders depending on circumstances, please read entire **Quilting** section, pages 61 – 63, before beginning project.*

TYPES OF QUILTING DESIGNS

In the Ditch Quilting
Quilting along seamlines or along edges of appliquéd pieces is called "in the ditch" quilting. This type of quilting should be done on side **opposite** seam allowance and does not have to be marked.

Outline Quilting
Quilting a consistent distance, usually ¹/₄", from seam or appliqué is called "outline" quilting. Outline quilting may be marked, or ¹/₄" masking tape may be placed along seamlines for quilting guide. (Do not leave tape on quilt longer than necessary, since it may leave an adhesive residue.)

Motif Quilting
Quilting a design, such as a feathered wreath, is called "motif" quilting. This type of quilting should be marked before basting quilt layers together.

Echo Quilting
Quilting that follows the outline of an appliquéd or pieced design with two or more parallel lines is called "echo" quilting. This type of quilting does not need to be marked.

Meandering Quilting
Quilting in random curved lines and swirls is called "meandering" quilting. Quilting lines should not cross or touch each other. This type of quilting does not need to be marked.

general instructions

MARKING QUILTING LINES

Quilting lines may be marked using fabric marking pencils, chalk markers, or water- or air-soluble pens.

Simple quilting designs may be marked with chalk or chalk pencil after basting. A small area may be marked, then quilted, before moving to next area to be marked. Intricate designs should be marked before basting using a more durable marker.

Caution: Pressing may permanently set some marks. **Test** different markers **on scrap fabric** to find one that marks clearly and can be thoroughly removed.

A wide variety of pre-cut quilting stencils, as well as entire books of quilting patterns, are available. Using a stencil makes it easier to mark intricate or repetitive designs.

To make a stencil from a pattern, center template plastic over pattern and use a permanent marker to trace pattern onto plastic. Use a craft knife with single or double blade to cut channels along traced lines (**Fig. 13**).

PREPARING THE BACKING

To allow for slight shifting of quilt top during quilting, backing should be approximately 2" larger on all sides for baby and wall quilts, and 4" larger for throws and bed quilts. Yardage requirements listed for quilt backings are calculated for 43"/44"w fabric. Using 90"w or 108"w fabric for the backing of a bed-sized quilt may eliminate piecing. To piece a backing using 43"/44"w fabric, use the following instructions.

1. Measure length and width of quilt top; add 4" (or 8") to each measurement.
2. Cut backing fabric into two lengths slightly longer than determined *length* measurement. Trim selvages. Place lengths with right sides facing and sew long edges together, forming tube (**Fig. 14**). Match seams and press along one fold (**Fig. 15**). Cut along pressed fold to form single piece (**Fig. 16**).
3. Trim backing to size determined in Step 1 or specified in project instructions; press seam allowances open.

CHOOSING THE BATTING

The appropriate batting will make quilting easier. For fine hand quilting, choose low-loft batting. All cotton or cotton/polyester blend battings work well for machine quilting because the cotton helps "grip" quilt layers. If quilt is to be tied, a high-loft batting, sometimes called extra-loft or fat batting, may be used to make quilt "fluffy."

Types of batting include cotton, polyester, cotton/polyester blend, wool, cotton/wool blend, and silk.

When selecting batting, refer to package labels for characteristics and care instructions. Cut batting same size as prepared backing.

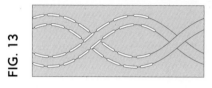
FIG. 13

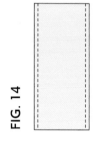
FIG. 14

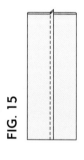
FIG. 15

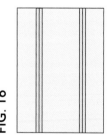
FIG. 16

ASSEMBLING THE QUILT

1. Examine wrong side of quilt top closely; trim any seam allowances and clip any threads that may show through front of the quilt. Press quilt top, being careful not to "set" any marked quilting lines.

2. Place backing *wrong* side up on flat surface. Use masking tape to tape edges of backing to surface. Place batting on top of backing fabric. Smooth batting gently, being careful not to stretch or tear. Center quilt top *right* side up on batting.

3. Use 1" rustproof safety pins to "pin-baste" all layers together, spacing pins approximately 4" apart. Begin at center and work toward outer edges to secure all layers. If possible, place pins away from areas that will be quilted, although pins may be removed as needed when quilting.

MACHINE QUILTING METHODS

Use general-purpose thread in bobbin. Do not use quilting thread. Thread the needle of machine with general-purpose thread or transparent monofilament thread to make quilting blend with quilt top fabrics. Use decorative thread, such as a metallic or contrasting-color general-purpose thread, to make quilting lines stand out more.

Straight-Line Quilting

The term "straight-line" is somewhat deceptive, since curves (especially gentle ones) as well as straight lines can be stitched with this technique.

1. Set stitch length for six to ten stitches per inch and attach walking foot to sewing machine.

2. Determine which section of quilt will have longest continuous quilting line, oftentimes area from center top to center bottom. Roll up and secure each edge of quilt to help reduce the bulk, keeping fabrics smooth. Smaller projects may not need to be rolled.

3. Begin stitching on longest quilting line, using very short stitches for the first $1/4$" to "lock" quilting. Stitch across project, using one hand on each side of walking foot to slightly spread fabric and to guide fabric through machine. Lock stitches at end of quilting line.

4. Continue machine quilting, stitching longer quilting lines first to stabilize quilt before moving on to other areas.

Free-Motion Quilting

Free-motion quilting may be free form or may follow a marked pattern.

1. Attach darning foot to sewing machine and lower or cover feed dogs.

2. Position quilt under darning foot; lower foot. Holding top thread, take a stitch and pull bobbin thread to top of quilt. To "lock" beginning of quilting line, hold top and bobbin threads while making three to five stitches in place.

3. Use one hand on each side of darning foot to slightly spread fabric and to move fabric through the machine. Even stitch length is achieved by using smooth, flowing hand motion and steady machine speed. Slow machine speed and fast hand movement will create long stitches. Fast machine speed and slow hand movement will create short stitches. Move quilt sideways, back and forth, in a circular motion, or in a random motion to create desired designs; do not rotate quilt. Lock stitches at end of each quilting line.

Attaching a hanging sleeve to the back of your wall hanging or quilt allows your project to be displayed on a wall.

1. Measure width of quilt top edge and subtract 1". Cut piece of fabric 7"w by determined measurement.

2. Press short edges of fabric piece $1/4$" to wrong side; press edges $1/4$" to wrong side again and machine stitch in place.

3. Matching wrong sides, fold piece in half lengthwise to form tube.

4. For **Blooming Baby Quilt**: Follow project instructions to sew binding to quilt top and to trim backing and batting. Before Blindstitching binding to backing, match raw edges and stitch hanging sleeve to center top edge on back of quilt. Finish binding quilt, treating hanging sleeve as part of backing.

   For **Yo! Quilt** or **Where's Everybody Going Quilt**: After trimming batting and backing, match raw edges and stitch hanging sleeve to center top edge on back of quilt. Bind quilt, treating hanging sleeve as part of backing.

5. Blindstitch bottom of hanging sleeve to backing, taking care not to stitch through to front of quilt.

6. Insert dowel or slat into hanging sleeve.

general instructions

BINDING FOR BLOOMING BABY QUILT

Blooming Baby Quilt, page 50, is bound with double-fold, straight-grain binding. The binding is sewn to the front of the quilt and folded to the back of the quilt.

1. Using strips for binding called for in project, sew strips together end to end to make 1 continuous strip.

2. Match wrong sides and raw edges of continuous strip and press in half lengthwise. Press 1 end of binding diagonally (**Fig. 17**).

3. Beginning with pressed end several inches from a corner, lay binding around quilt top to make sure that seams in binding will not end up at a corner. Adjust placement if necessary. Matching raw edges of binding to raw edge of quilt top, pin binding to right side of quilt along 1 edge.

4. When you reach first corner, mark ¼" from corner of quilt top (**Fig. 18**).

5. Using a ¼" seam allowance, sew binding to quilt, backstitching at beginning of stitching and at mark (**Fig. 19**). Lift needle out of fabric and clip thread.

6. Fold binding as shown in **Figs. 20 – 21** and pin binding to adjacent side, matching raw edges. When you've reached the next corner, mark ¼" from edge of quilt top.

7. Backstitching at edge of quilt top, sew pinned binding to quilt (**Fig. 22**); backstitch at the next mark. Lift needle out of fabric and clip thread.

8. Continue sewing binding to quilt until binding overlaps beginning end by approximately 2". Trim excess binding.

9. Trim backing and batting even with edges of quilt top.

10. Follow **Making a Hanging Sleeve**, page 63, if a hanging sleeve is desired.

11. On one edge of quilt, fold binding over to quilt backing and pin folded edge in place, covering stitching line (**Fig. 23**).

12. On adjacent side, fold binding over, forming a mitered corner (**Fig. 24**). Repeat to pin remainder of binding in place.

13. Blindstitch (page 66) binding to backing, taking care not to stitch through to front of quilt.

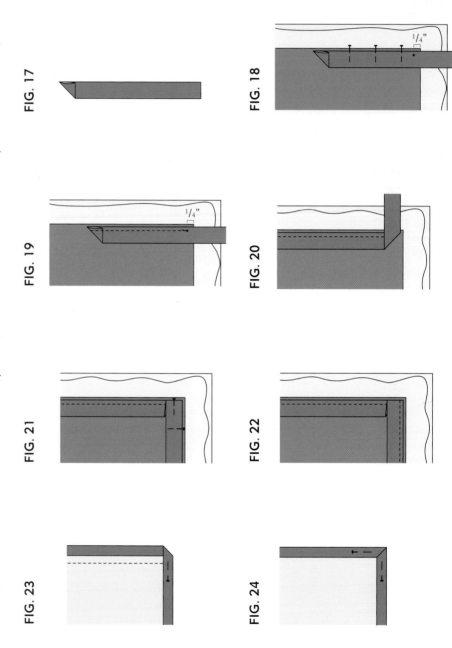

FIG. 17

FIG. 18

FIG. 19

FIG. 20

FIG. 21

FIG. 22

FIG. 23

FIG. 24

BINDING FOR YO! QUILT

Yo! Quilt, page 33, is bound with double-fold, straight-grain binding. The binding is sewn to the back of the quilt and folded to the top of the quilt.

1. Trim batting and backing even with quilt top.
2. Follow **Making a Hanging Sleeve**, page 63, if a hanging sleeve is desired.
3. Follow Steps 1 – 8 of **Binding for Blooming Baby Quilt**, except sew binding to quilt *back* instead of quilt top and fold binding to quilt *front* instead of quilt back.
4. Machine topstitch through all layers approximately $^1/_{16}$" from folded edge of binding.

BINDING FOR WHERE'S EVERYBODY GOING? QUILT

Where's Everybody Going Quilt, page 42, is bound with single-fold, straight-grain binding. The extra-wide binding is sewn to the back of the quilt and folded to the top of the quilt.

1. Trim batting and backing even with quilt top.
2. Follow **Making a Hanging Sleeve**, page 63, if a hanging sleeve is desired.
3. Follow Step 1 of **Binding for Blooming Baby Quilt**.
4. Press 1 long edge of continuous strip $^1/_4$" to wrong side. Press 1 end of binding diagonally (**Fig. 25**).
5. Follow Steps 3 – 8 of **Binding for Blooming Baby Quilt**, except sew binding to quilt *back* instead of quilt top using $^1/_4$" seam allowance.

6. On one edge of quilt, fold binding over to quilt top so that binding measures $^1/_4$" on back of quilt and $1^1/_4$" on top of quilt. On adjacent side, fold binding over, forming a mitered corner. Repeat to pin remainder of binding in place.
7. Machine topstitch through all layers approximately $^1/_{16}$" from folded edge of binding. Hand stitch mitered corners and overlap of binding on front of quilt to prevent gapping.

FIG. 25

SIGNING AND DATING YOUR QUILT

A completed quilt is a work of art and should be signed and dated. There are many different ways to do this and numerous books on the subject. The label should reflect the style of the quilt, the occasion or person for which it was made, and the quilter's own particular talents. Following are suggestions for recording the history of quilt or adding a sentiment for future generations.

- Embroider quilter's name, date, and any additional information on quilt top or backing. Matching floss, such as cream floss on white border, will leave a subtle record. Bright or contrasting floss will make the information stand out.

- Make label from muslin and use permanent marker to write information. Use different colored permanent markers to make label more decorative. Stitch label to back of quilt.

- Use photo-transfer paper to add image to white or cream fabric label. Stitch label to back of quilt.

- Piece an extra block from quilt top pattern to use as label. Add information with permanent fabric pen. Appliqué block to back of quilt.

- Write message on appliquéd design from quilt top. Attach appliqué to back of the quilt.

general instructions

HAND STITCHES

BACKSTITCH
Come up at 1, go down at 2, and come up at 3 (**Fig. 26**). Length of stitches may be varied as desired.

BLINDSTITCH
Come up at 1, go down at 2, and come up at 3 (**Fig. 27**). Length of stitches may be varied as desired.

CHAIN STITCH
Come up at 1 and go down again at 1 to form a loop. Keeping loop below point of needle, come up at 2 and go down again at 2 to form second loop (**Fig. 28**). Continue making loops or "chain" until reaching end of line. Tack last loop (**Fig. 29**).

CROSS STITCH
Come up at 1 and go down at 2. Come up at 3 and go down at 4 (**Fig. 30**).

DOUBLE CROSS STITCH
Working in numerical order, come up at odd numbers and go down at even numbers (**Fig. 31**).

RUNNING STITCH
The running stitch consists of a series of straight stitches with the stitch length equal to the space between stitches. Come up at 1, go down at 2, and come up at 3 (**Fig. 32**).

SATIN STITCH
Come up at 1, go down at 2, and come up at 3. Continue until area is filled (**Fig. 33**). Work stitches close together, but not overlapping.

STRAIGHT STITCH
Come up at 1 and go down at 2 (**Fig. 34**). Length of stitches may be varied as desired.

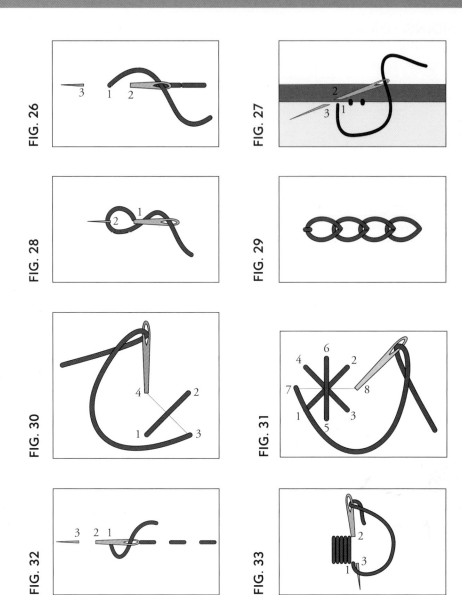

FIG. 26

FIG. 27

FIG. 28

FIG. 29

FIG. 30

FIG. 31

FIG. 32

FIG. 33

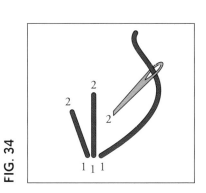

FIG. 34

Metric Conversion Chart

Inches x 2.54 = centimeters (cm)		Yards x .9144 = meters (m)
Inches x 25.4 = millimeters (mm)		Yards x 91.44 = centimeters (cm)
Inches x .0254 = meters (m)		Centimeters x .3937 = inches (")
		Meters x 1.0936 = yards (yd)

Standard Equivalents

1/8"	3.2 mm	0.32 cm	1/8 yard	11.43 cm	0.11 m
1/4"	6.35 mm	0.635 cm	1/4 yard	22.86 cm	0.23 m
3/8"	9.5 mm	0.95 cm	3/8 yard	34.29 cm	0.34 m
1/2"	12.7 mm	1.27 cm	1/2 yard	45.72 cm	0.46 m
5/8"	15.9 mm	1.59 cm	5/8 yard	57.15 cm	0.57 m
3/4"	19.1 mm	1.91 cm	3/4 yard	68.58 cm	0.69 m
7/8"	22.2 mm	2.22 cm	7/8 yard	80 cm	0.8 m
1 "	25.4 mm	2.54 cm	1 yard	91.44 cm	0.91 m

The fabrics in the Baby Bloom collection were purchased at
Blossom Quiltworks, Sherwood, Arkansas.

" *What* is art?
Nature concentrated."

— Honoré de Balzac

Photograph by Cheryl Johnson